ARTISTS IN TUNE WITH THEIR WORLD

Masters of Popular Art
in the Americas
and Their Relation
to the Folk Tradition

by SELDEN RODMAN

SIMON AND SCHUSTER   NEW YORK

Manufactured in the United States of America

10 9 8 7 6 5 4 3 2 1

Library of Congress Cataloging in Publication Data

Rodman, Selden, [date]
    Artists in tune with their world.

    Bibliography: p.
    Includes index.
    1. Art—America. 2. Primitivism in Art—America.
3. Indians—Art. 4. Ethnic art—America. I. Title.
N6501.R6   709′.181′2   82-661
                              AACR2

ISBN 0-671-25611-4

FRONTISPIECE

Apse of the Cathedral Ste. Trinité (1949). De-
tail showing tempera murals by Rigaud Benoit,
Philomé Obin, and Castera Bazile.

To
Maurice C. Thompson,

whose commitment to Haitian and
Mexican popular art over the past
five years has led to a revival of
the first and a revelation of
the second

and to

Roslyn Siegel, Bill Negron
and *Manu Sassoonian*
without whose help this
book could not have
been completed

In this book the parenthetical notation (fig.—) refers to a black-and-white illustration that accompanies the text. The notation (plate—) refers to a color illustration that will be found in one or the other of the two color sections.

Contents

Introduction   9

I Indian Arts of the Northwest Coast, Central Canada, and the Southwest   15

    1. Introduction   17

    2. The Northwest Coast   21

        Tlingit, Tsimshian, Haida, Bella Bella, Bella Coola, Kwakiutl   23

        The Living Tradition: Bill Reid—First of the Last?   26

    3. Central Canada   32

        The Inuit of Hudson Bay   35

            Pitseolak Ashoona   39

            Tookoome   40

        Norval Morrisseau   43

    4. The Southwest   47

    5. Other Indians, Other Ways   51

    6. Epilogue   54

II Popular Artists of the United States   55

    1. Introduction   57

    2. The First American Originals   58

        Erastus Salisbury Field (1805–1900)   58

    3. Blazing Lights in Dark Corners   60

        Henry Church (1836–1908)   62

        Clara Williamson (1875–1970)   64

        Frank Baldwin (1878–1964)   67

    4. Artists of the Black Experience   69

        William Edmondson (c. 1883–1951): Miracles I Can Do   69

        Horace Pippin (1888–1946)   72

        The Two Minnies   77

    5. Artists of the Total Environment   81

        The Artist Nobody Knew   82

        James Hampton's *Throne of the Third Heaven*   85

        Pauline Shapiro (1915–1972) and Laura Lynch (1949–   )   88

    6. Through Immigrants' Eyes   89

        Morris Hirshfield (1872–1946)   89

        Ralph Fasanella (1914–   )   90

III Afro-America: Haiti and Brazil   99

   1. Introduction   101

   2. Haiti   104

      The First Generation (1945–1957)   104

         Murals: From the Centre d'Art Jeep to the Cathedral Ste. Trinité   121

      The Second Generation (1957–1972)   124

      The Third Generation (1973–   )   130

         Arts of High Fashion   140

   3. Brazil   141

      Sculptors of Genius   144

      José Antonio da Silva   153

      Other Painters, Other Ways   158

IV Indians Once Under Spain   165

   1. Introduction   167

   2. The *Mola*-Makers of Panama   170

   3. Guatemalans and Other Central American Image Makers   175

   4. Grandchildren of the Incas   181

      Ecuador   181

      Peru   184

   5. Mexico   190

      The Huichol: Rediscovering the Tribal Soul— in Yarn   192

      Marcial Camilo Ayala and His "Aztec" Family   194

         Background   197

         Seminal Encounter: The Family   200

         Marcial   204

Bibliography   209

Index of Persons   211

Index of Works   217

Photo Credits   223

Introduction

ONCE UPON A TIME—even in this country and century, as a matter of fact, when as many Americans lived on farms and in villages as in cities—it was possible for an uneducated artist living outside the cultural mainstream to see life whole. To see it whole was to present it whole: without sentimentality, without inhibition, and without resorting to a private symbolism only he could understand.

Popular art was not then, as it is today, made only by people living in such exotic places as Hispaniola, Hudson Bay, the Amazon jungle, Bali, or the Balkans. In American colonial times and on into this century, anonymous limners, designers of *fractur*, embroiderers of quilts, carvers of gravestones, forgers of weathervanes, and others created a folk art nourished by piety and biblical lore. Just before the curtain of conformity fell, blanketing the lowliest sharecropper's shack, a few stars blazed defiantly in the still-visible firmament.

To be black in a time of pervasive prejudice was paradoxically advantageous, for few others were so cut off from the compulsions to keep in step, pursue the dollar, and save. No American painter depicted war and peace more vividly than did Horace Pippin, and no sculptor's expression was more direct than William Edmondson's. The despised immigrant was a wonder-struck outsider too, else Morris Hirshfield's erotic dreams would not have emerged so pure. But by the middle of the twentieth century the mass media had closed in. Except in his subconscious there were few places an artist could hide. And social scientists were beginning to question whether society could any longer afford to tolerate supermen. Unbridled freedom for the individual produced Wagners, Joyces, Picassos, but it also nourished the Hitlers and Stalins, whose egos fed on exploitation and war. Was that kind of social chaos too high a price to pay for *Tristan, Ulysses, Guernica?*

In any age other than ours, the idea of an artist being out of step with his environment, let alone oblivious to the high culture of his contemporaries, would have been preposterous. Many sophisticated artists, to be sure, have been ahead of their time, or in revolt against its abuses. Bosch set himself up as a connoisseur of evil. Michelangelo in his *Last Judgment* flayed all those in Rome who were making a mockery of Christianity—not sparing himself. Goya turned the terrible wrath of his burin upon all hypocrites, tyrants, and warmongers. But even those exceptional social critics among artists paid homage to the enlightened ideas of their age. Had it been otherwise, their images would hardly have been understood. For to cry out against what passes for the norm, the norm must be identifiable. Other great artists—the majority, in times of peace—have been more prone to accept life as they found it, projecting their visions of a reality more perfect than mankind in general could imagine, but not deviating substantially from the values most men were trying to live by.

Today, with "civilized" artists alienated from society, at odds with themselves, and spurning the very tradition and goals of art, it is not surprising that art lovers are beginning to turn away from the establishment. Even collectors are having trouble with such "investments" as a cubic yard of earth, a promontory draped in plastic, or a film of the artist eviscerating himself. But where to turn? The humanist art of the past, which was made to give joy as well as enlightenment, is in the museums. The highly stylized tribal arts of Africa and Oceania cease to be created almost as soon as they are discovered; nor has their fearsome iconography ever been really comprehensible to Western eyes. Folk art, the traditional craftsmanship among those out of touch with the educated élite in their societies, survives where it can.

There remain the *popular arts*—mainly but not exclusively products of the so-called underdeveloped countries—paintings and sculpture by untrained, self-educated artists close to the folk by heredity or feeling, who instinctively rediscover the secrets of the masters.

It is no accident that popular art is a phenomenon of the past hundred years. In earlier times, the gifted peasant or journeyman was either accepted in his community, becoming an apprentice in an ongoing tradition, or, if his habitat was too remote to bring him into contact with others, perhaps died unnoticed—for his work, after all, probably differed only in degree of competence from the typical art of his country. Only when high art itself had lost touch with the life around it did popular art begin to flourish on the peripheries of societies already fractured into rival camps of academics and outcasts.

Among the latter at the turn of the century it was Picasso and his friends who discovered the first popular artist, Henri Rousseau (fig. A). Some of them acknowledged Rousseau's genius for doing naturally what no amount of effort on their parts could bring off. It was, in fact,

A. Henri Rousseau, War. *Louvre Museum.*

I

Indian Arts of the Northwest Coast, Central Canada, and the Southwest

1
Introduction

Primitivism is sometimes mistakenly dismissed as crude or naive.... Nothing could be further from the truth. Primitivism is the product of highly sophisticated artists who carefully select both subject and style for deceptively subtle uses.

—The New International Encyclopedia of Art

PRIMITIVISM, that branch of popular art referred to in the definition above, is the word we apply to the arts of truly indigenous societies uninfluenced by Caucasian modes. Tribal artists are not aware of the works of Praxiteles or Picasso and would be indifferent if exposed to them. Of the three high arts created in this isolation in the Western Hemisphere—the arts of the Pacific Northwest, of Mesoamerica, and of the Andean cultures—we are concerned here with the first: its antecedents, its achievements, and its contemporary derivations in modern Canada and the western United States.

Compared to the primitive high arts of Mexico and Peru, Africa and Indonesia, the arts of the Pacific Northwest are benign in character. One could almost call this a "happy" art. Even when dealing with death—a major theme in all great image-making—the feeling conveyed is of a passage to a less competitive world. Fear and the exorcism of evil, those emotions that give to the arts of West Africa and New Guinea their ferocious intensity, do not dominate the sculpture and painted or woven skins of the Tlingit, Kwakiutl, Haida and other Indian tribes of the Pacific Northwest. One reason for this difference is in the extreme dissimilarity of environments. The fearsome jungles of Africa and Indonesia were inhabited by beasts of prey, deadly serpents, and myriad insects carrying crippling diseases. The tribes practiced cannibalism and their religious rites of propitiation (like those of the Mayas and Aztecs in Mesoamerica) required sacrificial victims—and therefore constant warfare.

Along the northwest coast, cannibalism and organized warfare belonged to such a remote past that by the nineteenth century, when the tribal arts of painting and woodcarving peaked, their symbolism and weaponry had already been translated into mythic dance and ornamental armor. The northwest coast of Canada from Vancouver Island to the Alaskan border has rightly been described as "one of the world's richest environments." Protected from extreme cold by the Japanese Current, blessed with plenty of rain, and so abundantly provided with salmon, shellfish, seal, waterfowl, berries, and wild vegetables that agriculture was unnecessary, no animals were ever domesticated. The Indians traveled by canoe only. So much could be harvested in a few weeks that leisure (in which to create art) existed for the greater part of the year. The enemies of olden times no longer threatened, and until the white navigators of the West began to drop in, no disturbing influences from outside interfered with the development of a peaceful existence and a homogeneous culture.

In the inhospitable icy tundra north and east of this favored littoral, the situation was different. Descendants of the same Asiatic migrants who had crossed the Bering Strait four millennia ago survived, but in too much hardship and desperate pursuit of game to have the time to establish a tradition of craftsmanship. Called *Eskimos* (Raw-Meat Eaters) by European intruders—but preferring, understandably, to call themselves *Inuit* (The People) today—they lived in sparse dignity, carving tools and occasional dolls and fetishes out of walrus tusks or caribou horn. It was not until late in the nineteenth century that a handful of enterprising outsiders discovered the innate creativity of these people from the Arctic Circle, and brought them abruptly into the world family of artists.

In the great plains to the west and south of Pacific Canada, the Indians for the most part were nomads. Settlements were few and once the Spaniards had introduced the horse, whatever arts there were graced the ephemeral weapons and bridlery of the chase. The most impressive works of art to come from these tribes of hard riders date from the nineteenth century when artifacts of wood, leather, beadwork, and weaving were collected and cherished in the museums of the white interlopers (fig. 1). Only a handful of true painters emerged.

Farther still to the south, in the deserts of Arizona and New Mexico, prehistoric cultures—less advanced than those in what is now Mexico but clearly related to them—were born. They flowered, only to be swept away. Like the Mayas of southern Mexico, no one knows whether they succumbed to conquest, disease, or climatic disaster. The name Anasazi has been applied to these builders of the mysterious stone "cities" of the canyons, whose engineering and ceramic artistry still arouse modern man's astonishment.

In the prehistoric stone pieces of the Pacific littoral, all the formal

1. Horse, Sioux Indians. Wood. Robinson Museum, Pierre, S. D.

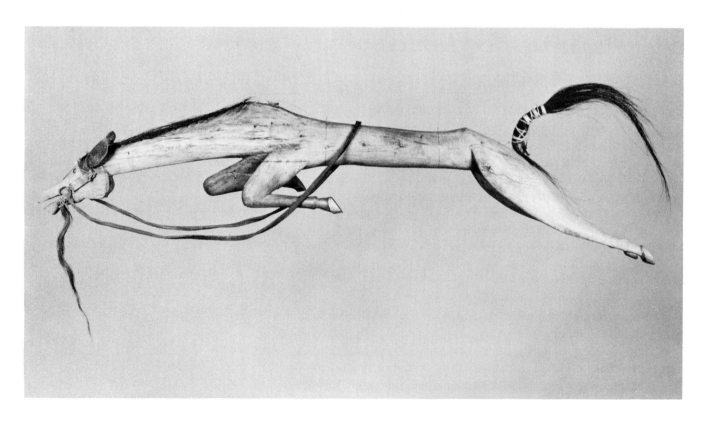

elements of climactic Northwest Coast art are to be found. Sometimes these sculptures are carved with such intensity that they seem to say: "You'll never know who we were, but you'll never forget what we made." The stone's intractability makes for pieces of unadorned simplicity, though the content of these archaic masterpieces reflects a fierce struggle for survival. All subsequent Indian styles seem to have germinated here. A grinning snake-skull figure recalls the fearsome Coatlicue of the Aztecs. A mother and child from the Bella Bella region foreshadows familial images of the Inuits of Hudson Bay. A hand hammer is as reduced to pure abstraction as any stone carved by Brancusi (fig. 2).

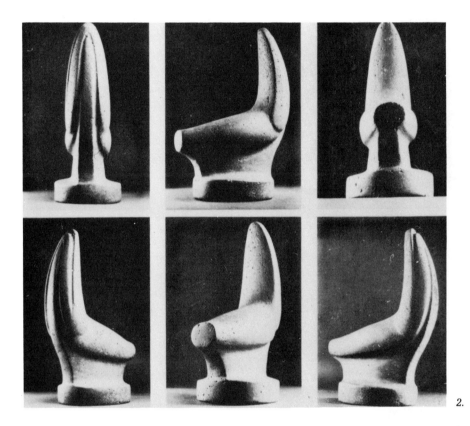

3.

2.

Wilson Duff, who writes about this anonymous stone art with romantic ardor, sees the medium's unyieldingness as consistent with the concept of wholeness, "too good for everyday use," made to carry man's symbols, "the medium of eternity." If a club could be devised to kill death (fig. 3), it would be made of stone:

> The phalliform pestle is the very image of man's power . . . but at the expense of its everyday use. . . . Art seems to deal with that which is terrifying and that which is taboo, and it does it in the guise of that which is familiar and controllable. We penetrate its guises at our own peril, and most of the time, the best common sense is not to try. But the terrifying and the taboo—in a word the sacred—will not be ignored, and it seems to be the mission of great artists to show us how to come to terms with them.

2. Hand hammer (slope-handled maul), Alaska. Images Stone B.C., Hancock House.

3. Hafted hammer: The Hawk that Eats Whales. From Images Stone B.C. (Duff). Hancock House.

To the aid of the writer's persuasive thesis came a happy discovery: two masks of stone from the Tsimshian region of the Alaska–Canada border, one with eye-sockets empty, staring (fig. 4), the other with eyes closed as though in sleep or blindness (plate 1). Though located in Ottawa and Paris, these two masks, while on joint exhibition for the first time, were found to fit one within the other so perfectly as to leave no doubt that they were carved by the same pre-historic hand. Such masks of "transformation" are common in most of the great primitive societies and will be described later in this book where they occur; but this pair is unique for being carved out of stone, and for presenting with disarming simplicity the duality of seeing and feeling.

4. Stone mask, Tsimshian. Basalt. Musée de l'Homme, Paris.

THE HIGH ART of the Northwest Coast Indians has been "discovered" twice in our time. As in the case of African sculpture, it was discovered first by ethnologists and anthropologists, and later on by modern artists who recognized a kinship with its free association, symbolic punning, and abstract quality.

Explorers, of whom the most famous was Captain James Cook (1728–79), were the first collectors of Northwest Coast Indian art. Traders sailing along the Pacific coast of North America in the late eighteenth and early nineteenth centuries picked up so many "Indian curios" that by the 1820s a substantial souvenir industry was thriving. But it was not until sixty years later that Lieutenant George Thornton Emmons, a naval officer whose father had been a Civil War hero, decided to devote his life to preserving what remained of this great culture. (That Emmons's mother and grandmother were mystics may account for this preoccupation, so unusual in materialistic post–Civil War America.) Appreciating the warrior reputation of Emmons's father, the Indian chiefs confided some of their secrets to the son. The American explorer wrote a monograph on Chilkat blankets (fig. 6). Among the Tlingit on the Alaskan border, he was told enough about the meaning of the symbolic designs to be able to help the brilliant young scholar Franz Boas decipher them. Emmons's first shipment of "specimens" to the American Museum of Natural History consisted of 2,775 priceless pieces.

2
The Northwest Coast

5. Three Brothers, Old Head-men of the Chilkat Tribe, Northwest Coast. *Photo by Case and Draper, 1907. Peabody Museum, Harvard University.*

6. *Chilkat blanket, Tlingit. American Museum of Natural History.*

Another notable collector for the museums, Louis Shotridge, seems to have been confused about his allegiance vis-à-vis the Indians and their often greedy and demanding sponsors. Understandably so, for Shotridge, a hunting companion of Teddy Roosevelt and John Wanamaker, was himself the son of a Tlingit chief (fig. 7). He tried at one time to buy the masterpiece of Northwest Coast art, the Whale House screen at Klukwan, northwest of Juneau, but failing to talk his suspicious fellow-tribesmen into parting with it, made a bungled attempt to steal it (fig. 8).

Nothing illustrates better the paradoxical status of the Indians and their art than the fact that the Tlingits later on turned down an offer to sell the screen to a museum for $750,000; and then, lacking the resources to protect it properly, let it fall into a state of decay. Only the great posts remain intact (fig. 9).

The interesting fact is that as a result of this stimulus imparted by collectors, Northwest Coast Indian art reached heights it might otherwise never have attained. Although faced with both commercial demands for greater and greater output—which it seemed would cause an inevitable decline in quality—and of a loss of faith in the institutions that gave them inspiration, artists like Charles Edenshaw and Joe Seaweed at the turn of the century created sculptures perhaps never surpassed in the earlier days of noncompetitive isolation; and today, as we shall see, a few of their contemporary counterparts manage to keep the flame burning as brightly.

The second "discovery" of Northwest Coast Indian art took place in New York right after World War II, and I happened to be among those who participated in it. As Co-Director of Le Centre d'Art in Port-au-Prince, Haiti (see p. 121), I had shared a gallery with the antiquarian dealer Julius Carlebach. I encouraged Carlebach to buy more of the pieces from George Heye's Museum of the American Indian— pieces assembled from the overflow of Emmons's horde at the American Museum of Natural History and the hordes of other on-the-spot buyers. Heye still called these sculptures "jokes" and was selling them

7. Louis Shotridge, Chilkat chief, in ceremonial robes. University Museum, University of Pennsylvania.

8. Whale House screen, Tlingit, at Klukwan, Alaska. University Museum, University of Pennsylvania.

9. Wooden sculptured posts, Klukwan screen. American Museum of Natural History.

to Carlebach for as little as $50 each. He changed his tune (and his prices) when he saw the avidity with which the surrealist artists—Matta, Duchamp, Haytor, Ernst, Tanguy, and others—now began to buy from Carlebach, to whom I had introduced them.

In 1946, when Betty Parsons decided to put on a show of this art and published a catalogue with a preface by Barnett Newman, Northwest Coast art, with the imprimatur of the establishment, was officially accepted. The New York museums, once they loaned pieces to the gallery's show, stopped referring to them as "specimens."

Tlingit, Tsimshian, Haida, Bella Bella, Bella Coola, Kwakiutl

The styles of the various tribes that occupy the islands and narrow coastal strip between Vancouver and Alaska are usually distinguishable—to an expert. To the layman, and even to the art critic, it is the similarities that are more striking. I showed the four 15¢ stamps put out in 1980 by the U.S. Post Office (fig. 10) to a knowledgeable dealer and asked him if he could identify by tribe any of the four masks—two Chilkat-Tlingit, the other two Bella Bella and Bella Coola. He couldn't.

Does it matter that the wonder-weaving Tlingits of Yakutat Bay and the Tsimshians to the south, across the strait from the Queen Charlotte Islands, used gill scales and mollusc teeth for their shamans' masks, sometimes adding Chinese temple coins for eyes, or topping them with tufts of scraggly hair? That the Bella Bella, a subtribe of the Kwakiutl on Milbank Sound far to the south, like the Haida used vertical and horizontal inlays of abalone shell to embellish the features of their masks (fig. 11)? That the Saltish-speaking Bella Coola of Vancouver Island placed corollas around the face, personifying Nukanoho-mih-Skalnaulti, the winged demon of the forest who influences men's thoughts?

All such considerations were absolutely vital to the creators of those works of art, and are fascinating to scholars, but are no more necessary to the appreciation of the art than a knowledge of how and why Mozart modulates from one key to another is required in order to be moved by the *Jupiter* symphony or the *Requiem*.

The two other major tribes of the region (none of them spoke a language that any of the others could understand)—the Kwakiutl in the areas north of the Columbia River and the Haidas of the Queen Charlotte and Prince of Wales Islands—have equally distinctive styles and have managed to preserve their ceremonial culture into this century more successfully.

Among the Kwakiutl, for example, old masks are still retained and used; and new ones, sometimes as finely carved, continue to be produced. Artists with great reputations, like the Kwakiutl master carver Willie Seaweed and Charlie George, Jr., of Blunden Harbor, emerged from anonymity at the turn of the century. Masks, Bill Holm reports, representing associates of the cannibal spirit Bakhbakwalanooksiwey, are still worn by dancers. Those personifying monster birds with

10. Postage stamps, four Northwest Coast Indian masks (1980). U.S. Post Office.

11. Mask with abalone-shell inlay, Bella Bella–Haida. British Museum.

12. *Dragon transformation mask, Kwakiutl. American Museum of Natural History.*

13. *Transformation mask, Kwakiutl. Painted wood. Museum of the American Indian, Heye Foundation.*

14. *Bentwood box, Tlingit. American Museum of Natural History.*

snapping beaks (fig. 12) are among the most spectacular Northwest Coast masks. "The masks as well as the dancers are hung with shredded cedar bark, some of it dyed red . . . the jaws hinged and rigged with cords enabling them to be snapped at certain points in the dance" (fig. 13). Holm, himself a dancer and singer as well as a fine artist, has participated personally in such ceremonies.

The wonderfully inventive carvers of Queen Charlotte, famous for their painted totem poles, possessed the only quarry of argillite (black slate) in the region and have carved masterpieces in the material, beginning with Charles Edenshaw and Isaac Chapman and continuing into our time with Bill Reid, whose works in this and other media are discussed further on.

The reduction of what is common to *all* Northwest Coast Indian art has been explained, diagramed, and applied to the arts of past and present by Holm and Bill Reid. The word they use to convey the system of expanding and contracting brushstrokes (or woven simulacra of strokes) that enclose and define mythological forces is *formline*. "The genius of Northwest Coast is that it adapts to any form. It was conceived as a decorative art, not in our sense but to express a symbol while conforming to the shape decorated. . . . Men utilize what they have in hand to express their personalities. Northwest Coast artists *used the structure of art itself* [my italics]. So you get both very open and very concentrated formlines . . . the unlimited imagination of an artist pitted against the conventions he's forced to work within" (plate 5, fig. 14).

Formlines were used, as Allen Wardwell and others have pointed out, to convey meaning. Reliance on the ovoid form, bilateral symmetry, "splitting" of animal shapes, double meanings (visual puns), exaggeration of teeth, beaks, claws, are all elements incorporated by the calligraphic line which swells or diminishes to give dynamic meaning to the whole. Holm, as already noted, compares formlines to the rhythms of the dance, and points out that the best dancers were often the best artists. "The extreme abstraction of some of these patterns," Wardwell writes, "was dictated in part by the standardized and rigid rules of design . . . or deliberately standardized to conform to owners' ownership of many different crest designs, thus easily identifiable for his guests."

Writing about the remote ancestors of these artists, whose works in stone alone have survived, Wilson Duff describes the same system of formlines (fig. 15). He calls it an art of "stylized ways of representing animal forms, these serving the purpose of family crests and referring back to myths. The deeper meanings, the conceptual dualism inherent in such objects as a phalliform pestle, the owl which sees in darkness, the seemingly sexless frog which multiplies with every rain, the images that are both male and female, are what the formlines were designed to enclose, amplify and symbolize." The death-dealing club (see fig. 3), Duff surmises, may have its own deeper meaning.

But what did the latter-day Indians of the Northwest Coast—those whom Emmons, Boas, and later savants like Duff, Holm, and Reid could actually talk with—have in mind? Before the collapse of the apprentice system around 1900, there were artists well aware—or shall we say as aware as artists ever can be—of what they were doing. And a few of them had transmitted their secrets to other artists still living when Boas, Holm et al came along. Freed from the demands of mere economic subsistence, unburdened by war, families vied with one another at big feasts called *potlatches*. Excess food was sometimes ostentatiously burned. Not burned the way our wasteful materialistic society burns wheat to keep the price high, or the way the European Economic Community recently destroyed vegetables in a time of worldwide starvation, but burned to express a family's largesse and indifference to wealth. Why did the Tlingits boastfully pile up thousands of artfully woven blankets only to give them away? Why did the Kwakiutl vie with one another in smashing their copper weapons and tools? Was it a kind of substitute for war, our own ultimate solution to the horror of abundance? "A fighting with property," two modern social scientists in England call it. "Westerners tried in vain to stamp out this 'barbarous' contempt of wealth for wealth's sake, striking as it did at the heart of Victorian ideology. . . . By setting a limit to the accumulation of wealth, the potlatch gave meaning to it; whereas in the West there is nothing left but to get richer."

Thus at elaborate ceremonies designed to impress and excite envy, objects blazoned with the family crest were displayed. Totem poles of red and yellow cedar, piling crest upon crest, painted as well as carved, rose higher and higher. House fronts and screens could be as elaborate as medieval *reredos* and pulpits. Bentwood boxes, similarly painted, displayed the family's unworn ceremonial clothing. And what clothing! If any garment more gorgeous than the beaded Chilkat blanket of the Tlingits, embellished with sprigs of ermine and sealskin, has ever been devised, one would have to go as far south as the Mayas of Guatemala or the Incas of Peru to find it.

And every utilitarian object, from the canoe with its carved and inlaid prow to a soup ladle which imitated the canoe's shape, bore the inherited clan emblems—raven, frog, bear, eagle, wolf, whale, mosquito, or walrus as the case might be.

Other works of art among these gifted tribes had more esoteric uses, of course, though the formlines used to define them were the same. The shamans, like the Haitian *houngans*, used them to heal the

15. *Tobacco mortar (beaver), prehistoric Haida. From* Images Stone B.C. *(Duff). Hancock House.*

16. Formlines. Painted screens and houseposts (after Shotridge). University Museum, University of Pennsylvania.

sick as well as to exorcise evil. Masks, especially among the Kwakiutl, were used in initiation rites: the youths, isolated for months and "possessed" (as in Haitian *vaudou* or Brazilian *candomblé*) by animal spirits, shed their disguises to join adult society, purified, transformed. The transformation mask, as among the Indians of Mexican Guerrero, is the most complex achievement of Northwest Coast Indian art. But as in all classic styles the ultimate image (plate 5, fig. 16) is unclassifiable, a paradigm of the tragedy and nobility of man.

The Living Tradition: Bill Reid— First of the Last?

> *The only way tradition can be carried on is to keep inventing new things.*
> —ROBERT DAVIDSON, *Haida carver*

"At the end of the Nineteenth Century," writes Allen Wardwell, "the Indian cultures of the Northwest Coast were in a state of final decline. The last great age of chiefs and shamans, which had actually been stimulated by the coming of the European, American and Russian traders, was being brought to an end by the imposition of an incompatible culture."

True or false? True only in the most general historical sense. Untrue because the sovereign artist with his indifference to history and his sixth sense for making the tradition, whatever the state of its health or decline, conform to his genius, makes art out of what he finds. The Italian Renaissance "ended" with Michelangelo's muscle-bound athletes writhing in agony: overpowering, inimitable, *finito!* Did Caravaggio care? He picked up the pieces, added shadows to conform to his criminal taste for brawls in the dimly lit "discos" of his time, and started all over again. The intensity of his sense of drama changed the nature of painting.

Bill Reid didn't create anything or even think of himself as an artist until he was in his twenties. "I was actually in my early teens before I became conscious of the fact that I was anything other than an average Caucasian North American." His mother happened to be a Haida Indian whose parents had lived in Skidegate Mission, Queen Charlotte Islands, and whose father had actually lived and worked as a boy with the great Charles Edenshaw. "But my mother had learned the major lesson taught the native peoples of our hemisphere during the first half of this century, that it was somehow sinful and debased to be, in white terms, an 'Indian,' and she certainly saw no reasons to pass any pride in that part of their heritage on to her children." It was his interest in some of his mother's Haida bracelets, however, that awoke the young man's curiosity and drove him to visit the islands. Once there, he got to know his grandfather. "He spoke little English and of course I spoke no Haida, so communication was difficult, but I did learn that he was in fact the last in a direct line of silversmiths."

Before leaving the broadcasting industry—in which he was already a promising figure, with his deep, resonant voice and charismatic personality—Reid put his new convictions to work, writing and narrating a TV documentary about how the last of the totem poles was saved, and making a film record, *People of the Potlatch,* for a big exhibit of Northwest Coast art at the Vancouver Art Gallery. Then he set to work carving, turning himself into the artist he no doubt always was. While still working in radio for CBC he had studied jewelry-making at the Ryerson Institute of Technology (fig. 17); now he apprenticed himself in a diamond and platinum workshop.

Returning to the West Coast, Reid next became involved in a three-year project, re-creating with the help of Kwakiutl carver Douglas Cranmer a section of a Haida village for the University of British Columbia. After returning to jewelry-making again, he was next

17. Bill Reid, gold bracelet with dogfish motif. Collection Mrs. David Scott, Vancouver.

18. Bill Reid, Haida Village Project.

19. Bill Reid, Haida Village Project. Commercial Illustrators, Ltd. Courtesy Bill Reid.

20A. Bill Reid, beaver memorial pole (Haida Village Project), detail.

20B. Bill Reid, grizzly bear (Haida Village Project). Commercial Illustrators, Ltd. Courtesy Bill Reid.

commissioned by the Shell Oil Company in London, England, to make a totem pole—a pole so magnificently out of place that it was donated forthwith to the Skidegate Mission. In 1966 Reid played a leading role in selecting pieces from museums and private collections for "Arts of the Raven," at that time the most comprehensive exhibit of Northwest Coast art ever assembled. Some of his own pieces were included in this show, including the totem pole now in the University of British Columbia collection (plate 6, figs. 18–20). For the centennial year (Expo

18.

19.

20A.   20B.

'67, Montreal) Reid had already created a large gold casket surmounted by an eagle (fig. 21) and was commissioned to carve a seven-foot-square screen for the Provincial Museum in Victoria (fig. 22). There followed a year in Europe assimilating the sculptural techniques of modern art, an experience that deepened his own work and freed it from a too-rigid adherence to the Indian past. Returning to Montreal, Reid worked simultaneously in all the media of his craft: stone and argillite, silver and gold (fig. 23), wood and printmaking—excelling in all

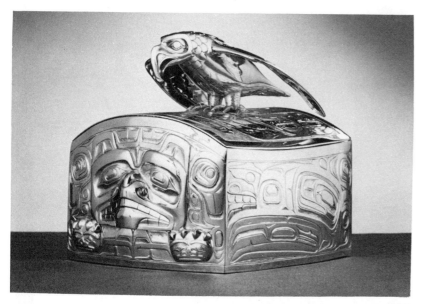

21.

23.

21. Bill Reid, gold casket.

22. Bill Reid, screen. Laminated red cedar. Commissioned for Provincial Museum, British Columbia.

23. Bill Reid, Bear Mother bowl. Gold. National Museum of Man, National Museums of Canada.

22.

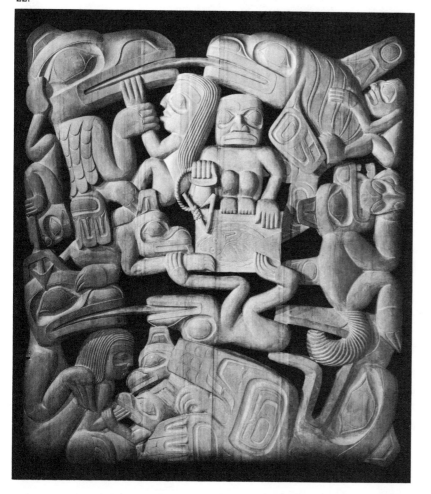

24.

25.

26.

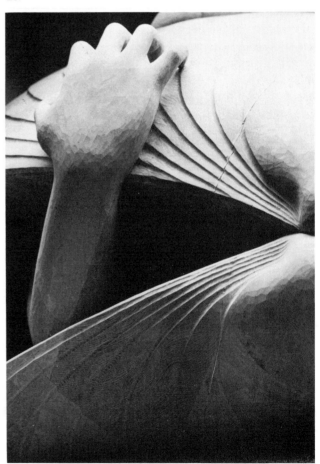

27.

of them. In 1974 he received the valuable Molson Award for his contribution to the arts, and completed a fifty-five-foot totem pole for his mother's village, the first to be erected there in over a hundred years.

What Bill Reid discovered for himself in the art of his ancestors is contained in his description of Northwest Coast Indian art:

> It is easy to become entranced by the soft curtain of age, seeing this instead of what it obscures. An ugly building can make a beautiful ruin, and a beautiful mask, in the dark of many years, softened by wear, becomes a symbol which tells us that the cycle of life, death, decay and rebirth is a natural and beautiful one. This is not what their creators intended. These were objects of bright pride, to be admired in the newness of their crisply carved line, the powerful flow of sure elegant curves and recesses—yes, and in the brightness of fresh paint. They told the people of the completeness of their culture, the continuing lineages of the great families, their closeness to the magic world of universal myth and legend.

Sometimes there is no perceptible distance between what Reid creates and the art of his ancestors (plate 3). But the daring innovation the sculptor brought to his perception of the inner meaning of the art of the past is revealed in the tiny wood carving *Raven Discovering Mankind in the Clamshell* (figs. 24–27). As noted in the introduction to the Holm-Reid dialogues, this piece "is pure Haida, but like no other Haida carving. It's monumental, yet only a few inches high. It's newly carved by a man we know, yet belongs to the distant past and another reality. Its intricacy, its compressed power, its tense relationship between Man and Raven, all these express—in Bill's own words—the precariousness of a society so highly structured, so highly developed."

Reid himself, talking to Holm about a tiny piece of Northwest Coast tribal art, uses almost the same words: "This is what makes it: this tremendous compressed power . . . no matter what the scale . . . this crazy mystique of the object inside the wood . . . the *courage* to take it beyond the point your mind tells you is logical."

Quoting Buckminster Fuller's guess that all technology derives from the sea, Reid enlarges upon the perception that a carved wooden ladle is based on the shape of the canoe:

> Its beauty derives from its function. If it looks good, it is good. That's a primary rule of all technology. They [the Indians] were trained, skilled, talented professionals. A professional artist requires a corresponding audience and body of critics. Otherwise there really can't be professional artists—men who produce things desired enough to be commissioned. . . . An artist in a rigidly structured society must express his individuality to the utmost, but within that structure. Men utilize what they have at hand to express their personalities. Northwest Coast art used the structure of art itself. So you get both very open and very concentrated formlines . . . the unlimited imagination of an artist pitted against the conventions he's forced to work within. . . .

24, 25. Bill Reid, Raven and the First Men. *First carved in wood 2–3″ high, later from a 4½-ton block of cedar for the Museum of Anthropology, University of British Columbia.*

26, 27. Raven and the First Men: *details.*

3
Central Canada

SHORTLY AFTER WORLD WAR II, the Canadian government began herding its 23,000 Eskimos, as they were then called, into permanent settlements. One such was the abandoned U.S. air base at Frobisher Bay. The idea was to take a census and bring these nomads some of the "benefits" of civilization. The idea of exploiting the Indians' craft skills came later. Except for those who were to prosper as artists, the original transplantation was a disaster. The family structure broke down. Fathers, relieved of the responsibility of supporting their families by hunting and fishing, accepted welfare and took to drink. Children, who had once done the family chores and acquired craft skills, were sent to schools, sometimes hundreds of miles from home for months at a time, where they learned English. There is on record the case of an Indian woman with fresh seal in the icebox who lived on frozen pizza and licorice sticks. "We went overnight from zero to satellite TV," one young man said. "How can you know what's real and unreal, let alone what's good or bad?"

In the far north around Spence Bay at that time there were still a few practicing *ankakoks* (shamans) who made "magic" fetishes out of whalebone. Their ancestors, spreading eastward from Greenland, had encountered neolithic Eskimos (Cape Dorset culture) who incised fine-line designs on ivory (fig. 28), often depicting whale hunters in their *umiaks* (skin boats). Intruders from "Thule" had invented the bow-drill but they were poorer artists. Through the eighteenth and nineteenth centuries their descendants were still making a few nonutilitarian objects and selling them to European navigators. The word *Takuminatuk* (that which wants to be looked at; fidelity to life) describes their realism. Only the alienated made abstract works to symbolize their dreams of the past or future.

By the forties and fifties of this century the word Inuit had taken hold and began to be applied to the settlements around Hudson Bay and as far to the north of that huge sea as Baffin Island and Baker Lake. It was in 1948 that a Canadian artist, James Houston, encouraged the Inuit to make soapstone carvings depicting fishing and hunting activities as their fathers had practiced them. Hundreds of the attractive small pieces were taken to Montreal and sold there (fig. 29). The Canadian government then set up the Canadian Handicraft Guild and the Hudson's Bay Company sold the carvings at local trading posts. Taking his cue from the incised whalebones, Houston established the first

28. Incised pipestem, Alaska Eskimo. Walrus ivory. Smithsonian Institution.

29. Family group displaying fish, Inuit. Soapstone. Collection Dr. and Mrs. Bernard Wagner.

28.

29.

graphic arts print studio at Cape Dorset. A little later another Canadian artist, Jack Butler, and his wife, Sheila, established the Baker Lake Printmakers, who combined stencil and stone cuts, producing editions of twenty-four to forty expertly made prints for the now-eager Canadian market. Soon the printmakers were branching out into wall-hangings (fig. 30). The independent cooperative they formed was called *sanavik* (a place to work). The government of the Northwest Territory put the Butlers on their payroll. In the sixties, following shows in New York and Washington as well as in Toronto and Ottawa, the works of such printmakers from Baker Lake as Oonark, Tavinick, Tookoome, Iksiqtaaryuk/Kenak, Ananaisee, and Turulialik—joined by Pitseolak and Kenojuak from Cape Dorset—became highly prized in Canada (fig. 31).

30. Jessie Oonark, felt and wool screen. National Arts Center, Ottawa.

31. Ananaisee Alkatukt, Family of Mermaids. Canadian Ethnology Service, National Museum of Man, National Museums of Canada.

30.

31.

The Eskimo language has no word for *art* or *artist*. Realism, but realism interpreted with poetry and fantasy, continued to be the aesthetic of Inuit art. "One must like it, since it is true," said one carver. "To be beautiful means to succeed in being real." But there remains the mystery of why art assumed vitality in places like Baker Lake and Inoucdjouak but faltered in Alaska. Why did the Alaskan Eskimos stop making masks—masks sometimes as arresting as any to come from the Northwest Coast (fig. 32)—and turn to making dolls? (Their most popular export, "Billikens," were adapted from a vulgar figurine patented by a Kansas City, Missouri, art teacher.) Why did "Happy Jack" in the twenties imitate scrimshaw and western pictorial illustrations? Why were the artists apparently satisfied to turn out curios,

32. Spirit of Winter. *Wood mask with feathers. Museum of the American Indian, Heye Foundation.*

ashtrays, cribbage boards, and match-holders for the white man's mantel? Why was a program introduced in 1963 to provide power tools for the artists? Was it that no Houstons and Butlers were around to instill respect for quality and imagination? Ironically, perhaps symbolically, the last shaman of the Bering Strait area, Kuzshuktuk (Water Drop), died in the 1918 influenza epidemic after returning from a ten-year residence in a stateside mental institution. As late as 1975 an Institute of Alaskan Native Art was being set up—with non-native members.

What is to be marveled at is not that Eskimo art foundered on romanticizing an abandoned way of life and supplying the insatiable demand of Canadian collectors, but that in its printmaking it managed so often to rise above these banal images (fig. 33).

33. Fish with Rider, *Inuit. Canadian Ethnology Service, National Museum of Man, National Museums of Canada.*

The Inuit of Hudson Bay

The soapstone and caribou-horn sculptures and the stone lithography produced by Inuit people of such settlements as Inoucdjouak, Cape Dorset, and Baker Lake are not derived from an overpowering aesthetic tradition like the Northhwest Coast's. This art has none of the advantages created when the artist is "pitted against the conventions" as Reid describes. It has all the disadvantages of being directed, almost obsessively, toward an unseen audience of collectors looking for the picturesque. Its artists' very livelihood has been dependent on satisfying the taste of souvenir hunters with a fixed, romanticized implant in their minds of happy Eskimos hunting out of cozy igloos, a taste elevated only slightly by the efforts of museum curators to single out for praise what was most worthy. Perhaps as much as eighty percent of the sculptures produced have been motivated by nothing more ennobling than a desire to document a vanishing way of life: hunting seals and polar bears, paddling kayaks, inflating sealskins, and the like. Some of these works are inventive and formed with true feeling (figs. 34–36). But most are crassly realistic and sentimental. Only the work of a handful of printmakers rises above the level of competence. With these few, images, concepts, and symbols come out of a past so remote as to give evidence of a Jungian racial memory (figs. 37, 38).

34.   35.

36.

34. Bird, Inuit. Black soapstone. Collection Lois Diamond.

35. Fisherman inflating sealskin. Inuit. Private collection.

36. Iksiktaaryuk, Shaman. Caribou antler, fur, hide, etc. Collection Stanley and Jean Zazelenchuk, Baker Lake.

37.

38.

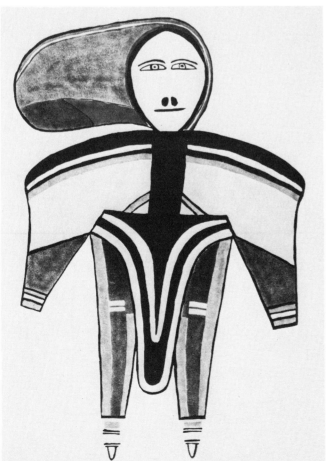

37. Tookoome, Musk Ox. Stonecut and stencil. National Museum of Man, National Museums of Canada.

38. Jessie Oonark, Figure. Wood, felt, embroidery floss. Canadian Arctic Producers. Canadian Ethnology Service, National Museum of Man, National Museums of Canada.

39. Pitseolak, Both in Summer and Winter.
From Pitseolak: Pictures out of my life, *from
recorded interviews by Dorothy Eber. Seattle:
University of Washington Press.*

40. Pitseolak, Dream of Motherhood. *Drawing.
Canadian Ethnology Service, National Museum of Man, National Museums of Canada.*

Pitseolak Ashoona

I first saw Pitseolak's work as I was leafing through a European anthology of "naive" art in which she was the only "Eskimo" included. She was described, misleadingly, as "perhaps the only one to have kept the true creative spirit of her ancestors." I was impressed by the one drawing included, and made a note that it had been taken from a book, *Pictures Out of My Life,* written by Dorothy Eber in 1971. The drawing depicted Indians with their pack animals, all attached by ropes, transporting their possessions beneath a horizon line shaped like an oxen yoke (fig. 39).

Pitseolak, whose name means "Pigeon of the Seas," was born near Cape Dorset where she presumably still lives. When Dorothy Eber interviewed her in 1970 she was already seventy years old, too many of those years spent doing what her people had always done to be in the slightest bit affected by the nearby telephone, upholstered couch, and plastic roses on the table, the inexorable "acculturation" of modern life. She had begun to draw following the visit of James Houston, the first civil administrator of West Baffin Island. His successor, Terence Ryan, established the West Baffin Island Cooperative. It was Houston, as we have noted, who encouraged the Inuit to become full-time artists and found markets for their work. He had also set up the first print-making studio in 1957. Pitseolak had now discovered her talent for drawing (fig. 40) and her capacity to take sustenance from the rich past that had lain dormant in her.

She remembered the shamans. As in Haitian *vaudou* (see p. 108), there were good and bad shamans. Bad shamans were consulted by people who had an enemy they wanted to put away. Pitseolak's father had almost been killed by a jealous shaman. People feared the shamans. "In the old days there were so many things to fear. I feared polar bears." Her father told her the tribal legends, like the one about the blind boy who got his eyesight back when a bird took him on his back and dived underwater with him three times.

"There were no teenagers in those days," Pitseolak recalled. "The young people got married so early they didn't have time to make any trouble." She herself had seventeen children, and two more by adoption. The mortality rate in those days was very high. "For boots we used only sealskins, and once the skin was cleaned we would chew it until the mukluks would be soft.... It's fun to chase a goose, and it's always fun to be around animals—they are meat." In the beginning Pitseolak made parkas and duffel sacks with designs. "Kitokshuk was drawing and I wanted to do drawings too, to make some money."

This was not Bill Reid's kind of motivation but it worked, at least superficially. "Jim Houston told me to draw the old ways, and I've been drawing the old ways, and monsters, ever since. Sowwik [J. H.] told the people to draw anything in any shape and put a head and face on it. He told the people that this drawing was very good. Some people, somewhere, saw the monsters, but I have never seen the monsters I draw."

The wonder is that Pitseolak, with this kind of advice, still managed to create images that have all the appearance of spontaneity (plate 7). Some talent is too indomitable to be driven off course, too innocent to be perverted.

Tookoome

The case of Tookoome, the stone-print maker of Baker Lake, is different from Pitseolak's, but my "discovery" of this artist was as inadvertent. Walking along Connecticut Avenue in Washington, D.C., one day in 1970, I glanced in a bookstore window and saw a color lithograph that I was sure was a new Picasso. A second look revealed the Arctic subject matter. I walked in and found a show of Inuit color lithos and sculpture. For Tookoome, the artist whose superb *A Time of Plenty* I then bought (plate 8), this had been his first exposure abroad. Up to that point my only confrontation with this intriguing art had been at New York's Cober Gallery where in the mid-sixties I had bought a spectacular print, *Arrival of the Sun*, by Kenojuak Lukta (fig. 41).

Inuit art came into its own with the print, and of all the printmakers Tookoome remains the most consistently inventive. One of the reasons for this consistency is that Tookoome has the good sense never to stray too far from his root-images. No matter how much he trans-

41. Kenojuak, Arrival of the Sun. Stonecut. Canadian Ethnology Service, National Museum of Man, National Museums of Canada.

forms them or fantasizes, the viewer is always comfortable, able to recognize some familiar object, man, or beast. As with Picasso, abstraction never becomes an end in itself. Picasso's distortions almost always "work" because the hand of the master draftsman is reassuringly visible. One never looks at a Picasso, as one so often does with those who followed in his wake, and thinks "the man can't draw." Tookoome's hand, in the more limited world he deals with, is as sure (fig. 42).

Take the case of the color print I saw in Washington, *A Time of Plenty*. A Canadian once asked an Eskimo what he wanted most from life. The answer: "I would like at all times to have the food I require . . . animals . . . then clothes." That is basic. But almost as important, perhaps more so from the artist's point of view, is the feeling in this statement by an Eskimo: "Life's greatest danger lies in the fact that man's food consists entirely of *souls*." In *A Time of Plenty* the souls are in abeyance, the bodies satisfied, even the seal joining in the benediction, on two *feet*. But in such a dramatic stonecut as *Quadruhuaq, The Mysterious Helper* (fig. 43), the eater seems to be paying the price for de-

44. *Pudlo, Man Carrying Reluctant Wife. Stencil. Canadian Ethnology Service, National Museum of Man, National Museums of Canada.*

45. *Niviaksiakik, Polar Bear and Cub on Ice. Stonecut.*

46. *Thomassie Annanok, Fisherman with Pail, Paddle and Traps. Caribou horn on wood base. Collection the author.*

vouring the "souls" of the fish and the deer by turning into a fish and sprouting antlers.

Humor, as with so many of these inspired printmakers, is ever present. The seal's feet in *A Time of Plenty* are a case in point. The humor of Pudlo's *Man Carrying Reluctant Wife* hardly needs its title to evoke a smile (fig. 44). Pitseolak's *Tennis Match* and *Dream of Motherhood* speak for themselves. Niviaksiakik's *Polar Bear and Cub on Ice* is as economic and irresistible as a Steinberg (fig. 45). More obvious is the Calder-like wit of a very recent piece, Thomassie Annanok's caribouhorn assemblage, *Fisherman with Pail, Paddle and Traps* (fig. 46).

44.

46.

45.

Norval Morrisseau

It was Brian Dalton, a young Canadian artist-teacher, who in 1975 suggested to the printmakers of Baker Lake and Cape Dorset that they expand their aesthetic horizon by looking at the outside world, forgetting conventions if need be. For artists as self-confident as Tookoome and Pitseolak the advice may have been liberating; but to jump the entire gap without falling on one's face at this point required an Indian with a superego, not afraid of making gaffes in taste, contemptuous of fashions, sure of his imagery (fig. 47, plate 9). That artist arrived on the scene amid cheers and catcalls in the early 1970s. He was an Ojibwa Indian from the part of Ontario that borders Lake Superior and his name was Norval Morrisseau.

Morrisseau had been around for some time, trying to find himself as a man and an artist. Possessed of unbounded courage and imagination, he lacked control and a sense of direction. Never in doubt about his own genius, he had so far convinced those who knew him only that he was a would-be Rimbaud, trying to push his body, his consciousness, his experience a little bit beyond the utmost limits of mortal possibility. There was no sign that he had heard of Stravinsky's injunction that "a renewal [read revolution?] is fruitful only when it goes hand in hand with tradition"—or that he would have profited by the advice if it had reached him. In fact, friends and well-wishers thought, there seemed very little likelihood that the reckless Ojibwa would survive the seventies at all.

As a boy he had bummed around, listening to the shamans of his tribe give their answers to the fundamental questions—who are we? Why are we here? What are we supposed to do?—but paying little heed. The tribal elders turned thumbs down on his attempts to "draw" their secrets; that was taboo. Could he have felt a sanction in the traditional Ojibwa method of disposing of an old man, inducing him to sing a death song and dance while the son came up from behind and brained him with a tomahawk?

In 1957, aged twenty-six, Morrisseau contracted TB and was sent to the sanitorium at Fort Williams, where he had visions. Some of these he carved in wet sand, knowing they'd be swept away. He experimented on paper, plywood, birchbark. One extraordinary drawing, which he called *Legendary Scroll Motifs*, contains the elements of his subsequent style, including the use of formlines and x-ray techniques, though less rigorously applied than in Northwest Coast art (fig. 48).

But Morrisseau was far from out of the threatening swamp of undirected violence. He was experimenting with every known drug. He was an alcoholic quite capable of killing himself or his friends, a paranoid personality drifting uncertainly between Roman Catholicism and the dying animism of the Ojibwas.

His life was saved twice. The first man to save him was the perceptive Toronto art dealer who discovered him—or rather, to whom he revealed himself—outside the shack made of old Coca-Cola signs that he had built for his family on the garbage dump at Beardmore, On-

47. Norval Morrisseau, Self-Portrait. McMichael Canadian Collection.

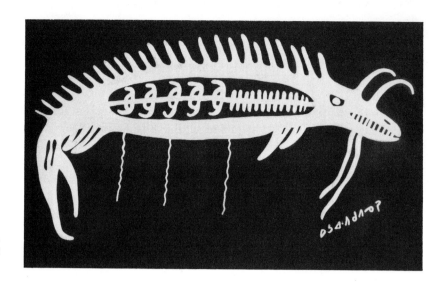

48. *Norval Morrisseau, Fish. X-ray drawing, white on black. From Sinclair and Pollock,* The Art of Norval Morrisseau.

tario. Until that moment Jack Pollock, who had heard of the wild man so obsessed by sin and guilt, had avoided him. But Morrisseau, with his great charm and unmistakable talent, won him over. Pollock offered him a standard contract which Morrisseau promptly tore up: "White man's papers are absolutely worthless." He might never have accepted the dealer's generous terms had he not become convinced that Pollock was part-Indian from way back. Pollock quickly recognized that this same outrage over injuries sustained by his once healthy and powerful people was not merely what drove Morrisseau to self-destructive turbulence but was as well the source of his creative fire.

Morrisseau's first show was an instant sell-out. A good review from Pearl McCarthy in the *Globe and Mail* alerted collectors hitherto educated only to the gentle charm of the Inuit. "He has realized," the critic wrote, "that though Ojibwa ritual laws demand that their metaphysics be kept secret, the Indians will benefit if outsiders know of their culture. And he has devised his stylized semi-abstraction to express the mysticism of the culture" (fig. 49). Overnight Morrisseau had become a celebrity, a culture-hero such as Canada had never known. (Bill Reid's sculpture had been too subtle, perhaps too intellectual and tasteful, to make this kind of a splash.) Morrisseau had bludgeoned his way to fame and fortune. Like Byron in London a century and a half before, he had awakened one morning to find himself famous. And like Byron's early poetry Morrisseau's painting was compounded of slapdash bravura and intriguing hints that the artist had secrets too corrosive and criminal to reveal openly.

There were indeed "secrets," demons within, that threatened to destroy Morrisseau, and he had to be saved a second time before he could settle down to pursue his career as an artist. As late as 1972 long bouts of drinking had led to a fire in the hotel where he was staying in Vancouver, covering more than half his body with terrible burns, but almost miraculously sparing his hands and face. In 1975 alcoholic dehydration almost finished him and he finally wound up (or down) at the Catholic detoxification center at Ste. Rose, where he painted *The Lily of the Mohawk* and other religious pictures that failed to satisfy

him or his critics. Like Reid, he kept remembering how as a boy "they brainwashed me not to speak Indian. Sin was my greatest problem. There is no sin with the Indian people. Indians don't have a devil. . . . I feel that I have outgrown Christianity. I wanted to make the Ojibwa feel proud again of their culture which had been taken over by the Jesuits." The commission for a mural for Expo '67 in Montreal bolstered his self-esteem, though this powerful work was subsequently destroyed (fig. 50).

50. Norval Morrisseau, Earth Mother with Her Children, mural for Expo '67, destroyed.

The ultimate salvation took the form of exposure to Eckenkar, a body of teaching centering around soul travel, which Morrisseau picked up after reading *In My Soul I Am Free*, a paperback promoting this latest cult out of California.

Whatever one may think of interplanetary soul travel, Eckenkar, as revealed in this simplistic pamphlet, was exactly what Morrisseau seemed to need, as both man and artist. As Lester Sinclair put it in his introduction to Methuen's big book on the artist, the new religion fitted very nicely into the Indian tradition of vision-generating shamans. Morrisseau, Sinclair added perceptively, is so self-assured as an artist "he takes what he needs. He is very quick to pick up new ideas he wants to use," and add them to a "mythology entirely personal and continually changing," as "blissfully self-centered and ruthlessly eclectic as Picasso ever was" (plate 10).

Morrisseau has made the Canadian critics and collectors as much his slaves as the Andalusian artist ever did the awestruck Parisians. Like Picasso's, Morrisseau's style is anything but subtle (fig. 51). It is made up, in his case, of borrowings from Northwest Coast and Inuit art, Mirò, and of course Picasso—especially the Picasso of *Guernica* and the Dora Maar profiles. Which is not to say that it is a style lacking in power, or that Morrisseau fails to live up to that image of an inspired madman he has created at great risk to his life.

51. Norval Morrisseau, Shaman with Spirit Helpers. Bayard Gallery, New York.

THE PEOPLE WHO SETTLED in the fertile river canyons of the southwest corner of what is now the United States arrived there two or three millennia ago and disappeared during the thirteenth century. Called collectively Anasazi, their terraced cliff dwellings display amazing engineering talent. They were an agricultural, peaceable people—which may account for their sudden extinction when the fierce Shoshones of the plains moved south. Their pottery came late; the best of it dating from A.D. 1050–1150, clearly displays Mexican influence (plate 11, fig. 52). The petroglyphs at Great Kivas, New Mexico, are strangely similar to the *vevers* of the Haitian *vaudou* worshipers (see pp. 107–108).

The great Mesa Verde cliff palace was discovered in 1888 by two cowboys. The discovery of the other abandoned cities in the Four Corners region (Utah, Colorado, New Mexico, Arizona) followed. The one at Chaco Canyon contained eight hundred rooms. Some of them are four or five stories high on plots of three acres or less. Most of the cliff cities were built between A.D. 900 and 1100, when the limited available arable land no longer supported the expanding population. But there had been time for leisure, time to create, and the pottery and jewelry were very fine. Then came the Spaniards with their diseases and sadistic religious practices and what was left of the Anasazi became dispersed. Their descendants are the tribes that inhabit the Acoma, Hopi, and Zuñi pueblos to this day. We know from their descendants that the Anasazi, like the Cunas of Panama far to the south (see pp. 170–74), were a matrilineal society, with the women owning all the possessions and doing the creative work. From the mythology of the Hopis we have the tale of Spider Grandmother sent to earth by Tawa, the creator, to show the tribes how to live together. It was one more case, as an anthropologist astutely put it, of "the wit and caprices of gods tinkering with man's perfectibility." What survives, after the great animistic figures of the Mexican-inspired Hohokam and Mimbres, is the craftsmanship of the Zuñis, Hopis, and Navajos, who carried that tradition of ceramics, basket-weaving, feather work and fetish-painting into the twentieth century.

Among the tribes in the Pueblo region, the Navajo were not only the most adaptable to the white man's ways but to this day remain the most numerous. And perhaps because they have always kept their rituals secret they have suffered the least contamination from the culture crowding in on them. Sand painting—or dry painting, as it is sometimes called—came closest to becoming a high art. Developed as a healing aid, to restore spiritual harmony within the patient, it was practiced (and still is) among the Navajo priesthood in conjunction with drama, poetry, and music (fig. 53). The most volatile of arts—like the *vevers* of Haitian *vaudou*—it has to be destroyed as soon as used. Its components are coloring agents such as cornmeal, pollen, pulverized flower petals, and charcoal, as well as sand. The soft-hued sticklike figures of the symbolized spirits (*yei*) are depicted frontally, but with the legs in profile. The paintings are stylized and static, but with some dynamism in the asymmetrical details. The artists work under an expert in the ritual. No fixatives are used, so that even had

4
The Southwest

52. *Two figures on a bowl, Mimbres culture. Museum of Northern Arizona, Flagstaff.*

53. *Navajo Indian sand-painters at work, New Mexico. UNICEF Calendar 1981.*

the paintings not been obliterated, most of our knowledge of them would have had to depend on reproductions or on their derivative uses on blankets or curtains for the tourist trade.

The pottery of the Zuñi and Acoma pueblos achieved superb results in the half century between 1880 and 1930. The traditional abstract designs are most in demand, but the innovative polished-black-on-matte-gray-ware developed by Maria and Julian Martinez in 1919 is very handsome too. The quality of the blankets of the Navajo, like the pots from the Zuñi and San Ildefonso pueblos and the basketry of the Hopi, was bound to deteriorate as the tourists' insatiable demand for them increased. A trash basket, a rug, a textile to fill a space on a wall or cover an ugly table—all were bound to become as banal as Polaroids.

Could the Hopi Kachina doll (fig. 54), the most desirable of all these collectibles, escape? Was there a "tradition" with which to conform (nonimitatively) or against which to rebel? The Hopi idol, so jazzy in color, so flighty in its dormant stance, was it a tradition that could survive? Perhaps. But because these feathered sprites symbolized an ambiguous spirit, they fathered no continuity. How could they, when condemned to live six months of every year on the San Francisco Peaks? How could they decide whether to be "spirits of the dead" or "cloud people"? Were they supposed to be intermediaries between the Hopis and the gods, or the gods themselves? No one told them! Were they supposed to make things grow—by singing, dancing, bringing gifts to children? Nobody believed them, not even the children who found them such fun to talk to or play with. No wonder they had no objection when the Indians began to mass-produce them for the tourist trade.

54. Kachina dolls, Hopi Indian. Collection Dr. and Mrs. Bernard Wagner.

Who were the Plains Indians and what do we have to remember them by? They were nomads and then warriors on the run; later denizens of "reservations" with all that that meant in servility and loss of self-esteem; and finally rebels whose newfound pride became sometimes too inflated to tolerate anything so "remote" as a work of art. For all these reasons, these Indians of the plain and desert created individual works of art but few artists who spent their lifetimes pursuing aesthetic goals.

Could Buffalo Meat, one of the prisoners at Fort Marion in 1875, who painted the superbly angular horse and rider with its touching attempt to achieve perspective (plate 12), have attracted any followers?

Could Silverhorn with his somewhat similar *Young Kiowa Brave* (fig. 55) have carried his art beyond spirited decoration?

Could Quincy Tahoma with his bravura buffalo hunter (*In the Days of Plenty*, plate 13) have surpassed this attempt to capture the prowess of his people in terms acceptable to the white man?

Does the anonymous artist who painted an Indian attack on a pioneers' camp (fig. 56) do more than satisfy our romantic notion of the hazards of life in the Wild West?

Altar-screen and *santo* carving was a Spanish folk tradition in

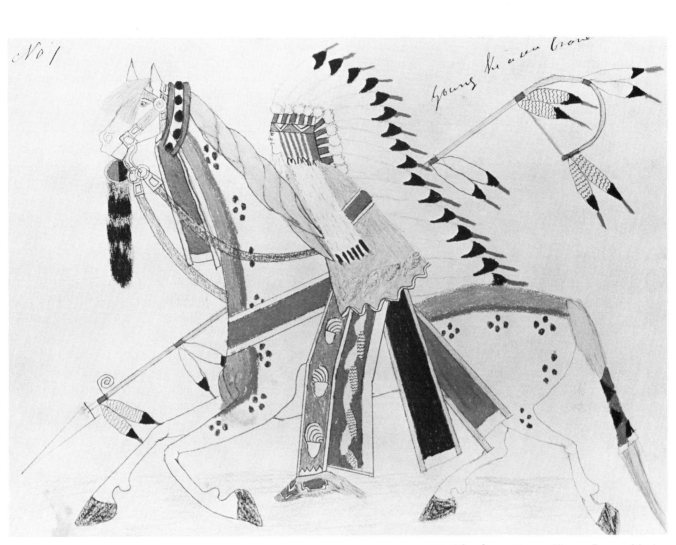

55. *Silverhorn, Young Kiowa Brave. Marion Koogler McNay Art Institute, San Antonio. Gift of Mrs. Terrell Bartlett.*

56. **Attack on Pioneers' Camp.** *America Hurrah Antiques, New York.*

New Mexico from the time of the Conquistadores until the first decades of this century. The master carver José Dolores Lopez began carving, the story goes, during World War I to allay the anguish he suffered when his eldest son was drafted to fight across an ocean on a continent he'd never heard of. He was the patriarch in a small village of Spanish-speaking Indians, penitents since colonial times when the state was a remote (and neglected) province of Mexico. Lopez was revered among the villagers as a good man, almost a saint. But at the same time he was shrewd, hard-working, and ambitious to see his large family well provided for with land and irrigation.

Since his father had been a highly skilled cabinetmaker, carving came easily to Lopez even late in life. A devout man, there was never any doubt about *what* he would carve: crucifixions, Virgins (like *Nuestra Señora de la Luz*, plate 14), and biblical scenes, sometimes enlivened by the artist's wit and portraits of the small animals he had made friends with in the isolated mountain valley (fig. 57).

57. José Dolores Lopez, Garden of Eden. Pine, aspen. Colorado Springs Fine Arts Center.

ABRAHAM APAKARK ANGHIK (Abe Ruben) was born in Paulatuk, Northwest Territory, in 1951, and studied silver-smithing, carving, and printmaking at the University of Alaska. The mood of cultural disorientation with which he entered college was broken by an Inuit teacher, Ronald Sengungetuk. "Sengungetuk taught me to look at art work as your life. The art is a reflection of yourself—a personal statement about the nature of knowledge." This lesson, which·Bill Reid had learned so well, and which every great artist understands instinctively, led Anghik back to shamanistic themes (fig. 58). The road back was not new and Anghik could boast of distinguished predecessors; Haydn and Béla Bartók, it will be recalled, had confirmed their genius for expanding the art of music by going back to Hungarian folk rhythms.

"The individual images are Eskimo," says Anghik of his sculpture. "Some of the totemic designs and carvings are Inuit (Hudson Bay). Some of Anghik's drawing, incised or inlaid on whalebone, looks as though it grew there. The striking head of a man surging out of an inverted totemic mask (fig. 59) was a feature of Anghik's first one-man show, in New York in 1980. But his work, like Morrisseau's, had first met with acclaim at Pollock's in Toronto.

5
Other Indians, Other Ways

58. Abraham Apakark Anghik holding mask. Bayard Gallery, New York.

59. Abraham Apakark Anghik, Shaman in Transformation. Collection the artist.

58.

59.

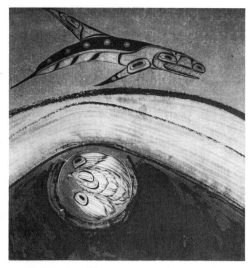

60. Ralph Aeschlimann, Guardian of the Egg. *Bayard Gallery, New York.*

Ralph Aeschlimann is a transplant into the Indian culture of the Northwest, an area into which this artist moved from Southern California very early in his career. He had previously served an eight-year apprenticeship in the art of the fluid Sumi ink drawings of Japan, which in turn the Japanese had derived from Sung Dynasty techniques in China a thousand years earlier.

Aeschlimann's *Guardian of the Egg* (plate 15, fig. 60) is the purest product of this cross-fertilization: Japan's contribution to Northwest Coast art, if you like, by way of the eye and hand of a true artist steeped in both traditions. "I've just taken something from the East and mixed it with the West," says Aeschlimann modestly of a recent exhibition, "so it's not distinguishable any more. To an Oriental it would look Western." Aeschlimann calls his birds "self-portraits with wings." Birds, he adds, are "aerial bridges that tend to be symbols of thought."

Fritz Scholder is a successful Indian artist whose motivation and

61. Fritz Scholder, Laughing Indian. *Oklahoma Art Center.*

background is quite different from these others'. Educated at the University of Arizona at a time when Abstract Expressionism was the rage, he was tapped by the Rockefeller-funded Southwest Indian Art Project, because (so he now says) "they wanted an Indian who painted non-Indian subjects, and I was it." Somewhat embittered by this patronizing call for his talent, Scholder began depicting the mistreatment of his people in a series of violently expressionistic canvases that gained appeal through his natural flair for color. "Sometimes older Indians will say to me, 'Oh why do you paint the Indian so ugly?' But beauty isn't cute or pretty. Ugly can be beautiful." It's a philosophy, or formula, that has made Fritz Scholder the leading influence among today's young Indian artists. The flat stylized images associated with Indian art in the past have given way, for better or worse, to Scholder's screaming, mutilated, distorted, but compelling, victims (fig. 61).

6
Epilogue

IT ISN'T IMPORTANT that these artists paint or carve "Indians." What is important is that they let themselves be turned on by their environment, by the folk tradition, by life. Yielding to nature, not fighting it, may be part of the secret. Scholars say that Newton's enforced rustication at Woolsthorpe during the plague year of 1665 may account for that surge of genius, never equaled in his life before or after, when he invented the calculus and discovered the laws of motion.

Exposure to elements of nature such as the forests, mountains, and pounding seas of the Northwest Coast aroused what was dormant in such urban painters as Mark Tobey and Morris Graves, who then visited Japan and became the kind of modern tone-poets we know today. It was when Bill Reid left the city to renew himself in the Queen Charlotte Islands that he became an artist. The pattern will be repeated as we move east and south along the orbit of popular art.

II
Popular
Artists
of the
United States

Long after the majority of her people either lost the leisure to shape their thoughts with a brush or a jack-knife, or put that leisure to less creative purposes, America retained her people's art. The years of democratic ferment had been those of her richest achievement in those humbler forms; but women in southern hills continued to weave bedspreads . . . and fishermen carved decoys whose sleek perfection an old Egyptian would have envied.

—OLIVER LARKIN, Art and Life in America

SO MANY ARE the varieties of popular art created in the United States during the two centuries of its independent existence that even to classify them is difficult. We have already commented on the art of the aboriginal Indians: pre-Columbian "intruders" from Mesoamerica, nomads of the plains and deserts. The English colonies produced their own kind of popular art, much of it surviving into the early decades of the independent nation, and all of it highly prized and well documented by such knowledgeable critics as Jean Lipman and Alice Winchester. Though the art of the limners and early sculptors is often closer to the rural folk tradition (fig. 62) than that of the artists we intend to feature here, it is a by-product of the English tradition diluted through its colonial transplants—less innovative and idiosyncratic for the most part than that created in isolation, whether the isolation of the country or the city.

1
Introduction

62. Mary Ann Wilson, Marimaid. *Watercolor. New York State Historical Association, Cooperstown.*

2

The First American Originals

THE FIRST WORK of art in the United States which does not lean heavily on the English tradition is Erastus Salisbury Field's aptly named *Historical Monument of the American Republic* (plate 16, fig. 63). The limners had relied on set formulas to convey the features of their Puritan patrons—compressed lips, almond-shaped eyes, hands in pious constriction. The middle class after the Revolution asked for poses a little less rigid. But it was no accident that the intensity of the Puritan expression was best conveyed by an artist unable to communicate with his sitters at all—the deaf and dumb John Brewster, Jr. The able Joseph Davies was also oblivious to personality, being more interested in such symbols of middle-class respectability as "the carpet, standing straight up under the tiny feet with a stylistic bravado." The even abler Jonathan Fisher is sometimes called, because of the many fields in which he researched indefatigably, "the Leonardo of Limners." He painted for pleasure, putting his portraits together with all the craft of an antiquarian but with a remarkable nobility of effect—the result of a profound respect for the value of learning (fig. 64). Noble, too, is the only word to describe the portraiture of Ammi Phillips; or the *Peaceable Kingdoms* of that most atypically contentious Quaker, Edward Hicks, who took the bold outlines, decorative borders, and lettered banners of the sign painters and made out of them a brilliantly colored symbolism for clients who rejected symbolism and color alike.

Erastus Salisbury Field 1805–1900

Field himself, the contemporary of these super-limners who outlived all of them, began as they did, painting conventional portraits for the big landowners of the Connecticut Valley where he lived. In fact the only trip he ever made out of rural New England during his ninety-five years was a visit to New York City, when he was nineteen, to study painting briefly with Samuel F. B. Morse. Perhaps it was the inquiring spirit of the future inventor of the telegraph that planted the seed of originality in the younger artist, but that is speculation. For it wasn't until forty years later, during the Civil War, that Field conceived and began to paint his masterpiece.

The history of the huge (13′ × 9′) painting (plate 16) is instructive and melancholy. Suddenly abandoning the exotic funerary pictures of pseudo-Egyptian and Turkish subjects that he had specialized in after the death of his wife, Field decided to make a work that would symbolize the nation's Centennial quest for freedom. There is no record that it ever hung in that year's Exposition of bad taste in Philadelphia. Partaking rather of the young Walt Whitman's "Song of the Exposition"—

Mightier than Egypt's tombs,
Fairer than Grecia's, Roma's temples.
Prouder than Milan's statued, spired Cathedral

—its seven Babel towers were linked by flying bridges along which the

64. *Jonathan Fisher, Self-Portrait. Collection Mrs. Robert L. Fisher.*

new steam engine, then opening up the West, puffed majestically. Reliefs and scrolls of amazing complexity on the polygonal walls depicted every major event and hero of the expanding republic. The eighth and central turret was dedicated to the martyred Abraham Lincoln and the Constitution, below which troops of proud citizens paraded in all their finery. Not until James Hampton, the visionary bureaucrat of a century later, put together his *Throne of the Third Heaven of the Nations Millennium General Assembly* (see pp. 85–87), would a work of such a mysterious, compelling complexity be created. Yet it wasn't until 1933 that the great painting was found, rolled up in the former home of Field's nephew near Springfield; and even in the 1940s it had to be rescued anew from a shed behind a pigsty in Plumtrees.

63. Erastus Salisbury Field, Historical Monument of the American Republic. Museum of Fine Arts, Springfield, Mass., Morgan Wesson Memorial Collection.

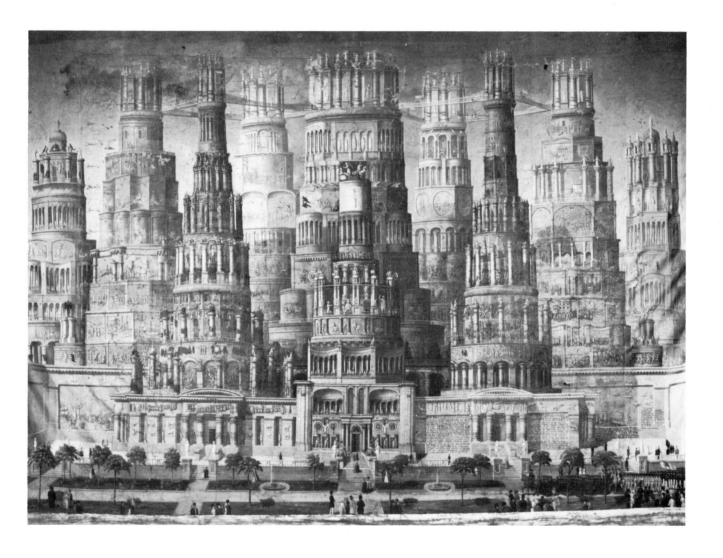

3

Blazing Lights in Dark Corners

FIELD WAS the oldest but not the last of the great popular artists who enlivened American painting during the nineteenth century and on into the twentieth. Some, like the inspired painters of whalers (fig. 65) and shipwrecks (plate 17), were anonymous. Some, like Olof Krans and John Kane, were immigrants from the Old World. Artists like Henry Church, Joseph Pickett, and Frank Baldwin were eccentrics, recluses who enjoyed no fame in their lifetimes and apparently sought none. Also without seeking fame, Clara Williamson, the pioneer Texan, lived to see her pictures exhibited and sold for good prices.

65. *Coleman,* Whaling Off the Coast of California. *Museum of Fine Arts, Boston. From Bishop,* Folk Painters of America.

Olof Krans (1838–1916) was one of the Swedish dissenters who established the Bishop Hill Colony in western Illinois. His memorable painting *Women Planting Corn* (fig. 66A) depicts the early days of regimented communism when the Devotionalists led by Erik Jansson worked eighteen hours a day planting their 2,000-acre tract—and built houses and storage barns in their spare time. Like all utopian colonies, this one dissolved in wrangling. Unable to compete with the free enterprise system about it, it fell apart in 1860. Krans's *Self Portrait* of 1908 (fig. 66B) shows the artist self-satisfied, marmoreal, sartorially splendid, but as Esther Sparks puts it, "with a glint of humor in the eye." It was probably, like his other formal portraits, worked up from a photograph.

How different is John Kane's equally striking and better-known *Self-Portrait* (fig. 67), a memory image of his early days as a prizefighter which simultaneously acknowledges the aging process that has taken place. Here is the artist literally stripped for action, intense, humorless, inner-directed, painfully self-conscious. When a degree of recognition came to Kane at the age of sixty-seven with his acceptance by Carnegie Institute's prestigious annual exhibition, the International, he wrote a letter saying he was too conscious of his failures as a man—his shattered marriage, his alcoholism—to be impressed by a

66A. Olof Krans, Women Planting Corn.
Bishop Hill Memorial, Bishop Hill, Ill.

66B. Olof Krans, Self-Portrait. Bishop Hill Heritage Association, Bishop Hill, Ill.

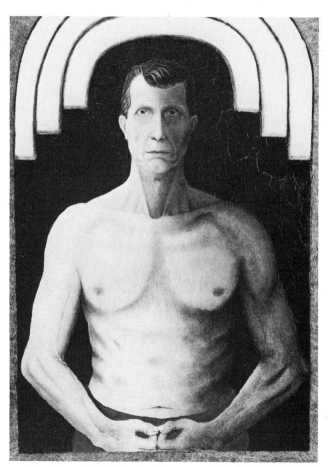

67. John Kane, Self-Portrait. Museum of Modern Art, New York. Abby Aldrich Rockefeller
Fund.

bauble. "When you walk the way of life with the poor, as I have, one honor the more, one rebuff the less, is nothing. I was proud and glad to have this recognition at last. But beyond that it was of little importance." Kane (1860–1934) painted not only Pittsburgh and the Monongahela valley—with a realism only an ironmonger, puddler, and journeyman carpenter could have achieved—but also the Scotland of his boyhood memories dating back a half century. "Search Vasari's *Lives of the Artists* from beginning to end," wrote Frank Crowninshield in the foreword to *Sky Hooks,* Kane's autobiography, "and you will find in them no more magnificent paradox than this: that an immigrant day-laborer who had no time to paint, no money to paint, no earthly provocation or encouragement to paint, should emerge, at the age of sixty-seven, as the most significant painter America has produced during the past quarter-century."

Allowing that the critic was not familiar with any of the other popular artists discussed in this part of our book, he was hardly exaggerating. Kane was such a compulsive artist that he drew and colored pictures on the sides of the steel railway cars he was building. "No artist," writes Kane's biographer, Leon Anthony Arkus, director of the Carnegie Institute's Museum of Art, "has equaled John Kane in portraying the industrial scene. Steel mills are organic, monumental structures; railroad tracks have a purposeful yet graceful sweep through his paintings; and houses cluster together as though they had sprung forth from seeds planted in close, orderly rows. Smoke pours from the stacks of factories and river boats, providing a dynamic contrast to the serene green hills. Kane transcended his technical deficiencies by breathing into his work a rare personal poetry. To judge Kane by academic standards is to rebuke Giotto for his lack of perspective or, more significantly perhaps, to decry the mystique of art itself."

68. Henry Church, Self-Portrait. *Collection Samuel and Angela Rosenberg.*

Henry Church (1836–1908)

Just thirty years after Henry Church died, the man destined to discover his talent arrived at Squaw Rock on the Chagrin River about twelve miles from Cleveland. Sam Rosenberg—photographer, artist, critic, surrealist and wit—had arrived just three weeks too late to prevent Church's daughter, then in her seventies, from burning all but a few of her father's paintings. "Nobody liked them," she said. "Nobody wanted them. I didn't want them to fall into the hands of anyone who wouldn't take care of them." No one will ever know whether two that survived, *The Monkey Picture* (plate 19, fig. 69) and *Self-Portrait* (plate 18, fig. 68), were the best or the worst of the lot, but few will deny that they are paintings of startling originality.

Rosenberg had driven to the Chagrin in 1937 out of curiosity, to see the seemingly unrelated carvings on Squaw Rock, overhanging the river: a child in a crib, a mountain lion hanging by its tail, a tomahawk, a skeleton, and a spread eagle "which might have been swooping down

69. Henry Church, The Monkey Picture. Collection Samuel and Angela Rosenberg.

to rescue the Indian woman from the serpent.'' Church's daughter told Rosenberg that the real name of Squaw Rock was ''The Rape of the Indian Tribes by the White Man'' and that her father felt such kinship with the abused aboriginals that he used to lecture from the pulpitlike rock to the spirits of the massacred.

An old man volunteered some gossip about the eccentric artist. ''Old Hank . . . carved out his own tombstone [a Peaceable Kingdom with lion] and then he preached his own funeral sermon on a gramophone cylinder.'' The cemetery trustees had refused to allow his ''ugly'' sculpture into the graveyard, until ''Old Hank'' threatened to live forever. He got even with them after his death when the funeral oration turned out to be a scathing denunciation of the trustees—and all other philistines. Henry Church was an eccentric all right, but surely not more of a one than Blake, Van Gogh, Gauguin or Ryder.

At thirteen Henry went to work in his father's blacksmith shop. His father, a deeply religious man, had paid $400 to escape service in the Civil War, though he'd been an ardent abolitionist whose home was a station on the Underground Railroad. He had also been an amateur painter, and made portraits of Lincoln and Sherman for the local Grand Army of the Republic, which promptly buried them in the cellar. And he had made musical instruments. Henry started painting, carving, and hunting the year his father died.

If ever there was a case of popular art deriving from folk art—no matter how lowly and aesthetically impoverished the folk—it is Church's two paintings. The ''inspiration'' for the *Self Portrait* was a before/after poster of 1865 advertising Wolcott's Instant Pain Annihilator, the face at the top of the ad registering pain while under attack from a swarm of little devils, one of which is sticking a spear into the victim's eye (fig. 70). It was the genius of Church to turn the demons into Muses, and the two ugly faces into his own thoughtful, amused one. *The Monkey Picture,* similarly, was derived from a coconut advertisement showing one monkey pulling the tail of another who has

70. 1865 advertisement for Wolcott's Instant Pain Annihilator. Courtesy Sam Rosenberg.

seized the only banana in sight. Church's genius in that case consisted in turning the banal Victorian still-lifes then saturating American homes into a satire on pretentious bourgeois décor, without sacrificing the sensuous flesh of the various fruits or the vitality of his three primates.

Clara Williamson (1875–1970)

Clara McDonald Williamson ("Aunt Clara") of pioneer Texas was the painter "Grandma" Moses might have been, had she had the talent—and the intelligence to resist the blandishments of art dealers who encouraged her to repeat endlessly those pretty picture-postcard Thanksgivings and snow scenes the public wanted. There were many points of similarity in the two painters. Both had been brought up in pioneer country. Both lived close to a hundred years. Both began to paint in their late sixties when relieved of the chores imposed by marriage and housekeeping. Both painted "happy" pictures. Both possessed personalities of great charm, characters utterly lacking in guile.

There the similarities end. Partly, no doubt, this was because Williamson's patron-mentors, Donald and Margaret Vogel, gave her a more rigorous sense of what good painting involved, but more importantly it was because her intelligence was equal to achieving what her eye and hand insisted she must do. Clara Williamson never repeated herself. Instinctively she planned her pictures to satisfy a sense of atmosphere, space, composition, and color as demanding as the masters' (fig. 71A).

71A. Clara McDonald Williamson, The Day the Bosque Froze Over. Museum of Modern Art, New York. Gift of Albert Dorne.

I
Indian Arts of the Northwest Coast, Central Canada, and the Southwest

1. Blind mask. Basalt. National Museum of Man, National Museums of Canada. Hancock House.

2. Figures on a bowl, Mimbres culture. Museum of Northern Arizona, Flagstaff.

3. Pendant. Copper, abalone, Queen Charlotte yew. Courtesy the artist.

4. Robe, shark with monsters, Tlingit, Alaska. Walrus hide. Museum of the American Indian, Heye Foundation.

5. Bentwood box, Tlingit. American Museum of Natural History.

6. Mask, Tlingit. American Museum of Natural History.

7. Bill Reid, *painted beaver pole. Totem Park Project, University of British Columbia. Courtesy the artist.*

8. José Dolores Lopez, Nuestra Señora de la Luz. Cottonwood. Taylor Museum, Colorado Springs Fine Arts Center.

9. Ralph Aeschlimann, Guardian of the Egg. Gouache on paper. Bayard Gallery, New York.

10. Pitseolak, Both in Summer and Winter.
Courtesy Dorothy Eber, Montreal, Canada,
from her Pitseolak: Pictures Out of My Life:
Recorded Interviews. *Seattle, Washington:*
University of Washington Press.

11. Tookoome, In a Time of Plenty. Color lithograph. Collection the author.

12. Norval Morrisseau, Self-Portrait. *McMichael Canadian Collection, Ontario. Jack Pollock Gallery, Toronto.*

13. *Norval Morrisseau, Warrior with Thunderbirds. Collection Helen E. Band. Jack Pollock Gallery, Toronto.*

14. *Buffalo Meat, Self-Portrait. Oklahoma Historical Society.*

15. *Quincy Tahoma, In the Days of Plenty. Southwestern Art Association, Philbrook Art Center, Tulsa.*

II Popular Artists of the United States

16. *Erastus Salisbury Field,* Historical Monument of the American Republic. *Museum of Fine Arts, Springfield, Mass., Morgan Wesson Memorial Collection.*

17. *Anon.,* Sinking of the Titanic. *Private collection.*

18. Henry Church, Self-Portrait. Collection Samuel and Angela Rosenberg.

19. Henry Church, The Monkey Picture. Collection Samuel and Angela Rosenberg.

20. Clara McDonald Williamson, Arbor Meeting. Courtesy Kevin E. Vogel, Valley House Gallery, Dallas.

21. Frank Baldwin, Crucifixion. David Wiggins, Tilton, N.H.

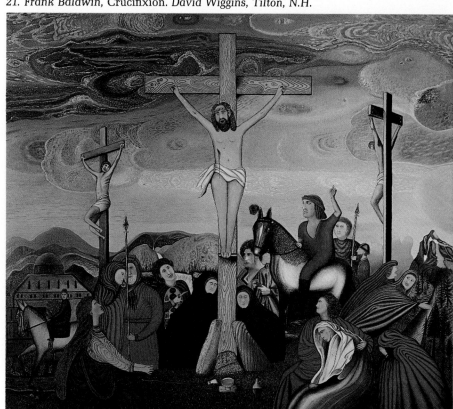

22. Horace Pippin, Domino Players. Phillips Collection, Washington, D.C.

23. Horace Pippin, The Barracks. Phillips Collection, Washington, D.C.

24. Morris Hirshfield, Girl in a Mirror. Museum of Modern Art, New York.

25. Morris Hirshfield, Girl with a Dog. Franco Maria Ricci, Milano, Italy.

26. James Hampton, Throne of the Third Heaven of the National Millennium General Assembly. *National Collection of Fine Arts, Smithsonian Institution.*

27. Minnie Deschamps, Church Service. *Collection Daniel Storper.*

28. Minnie Evans, painting. *RoKo Gallery, New York.*

29. Ralph Fasanella, Wall Street. Courtesy Eve Fasanella and the artist.

30. Ralph Fasanella, Gray Day. Courtesy Eve Fasanella and the artist.

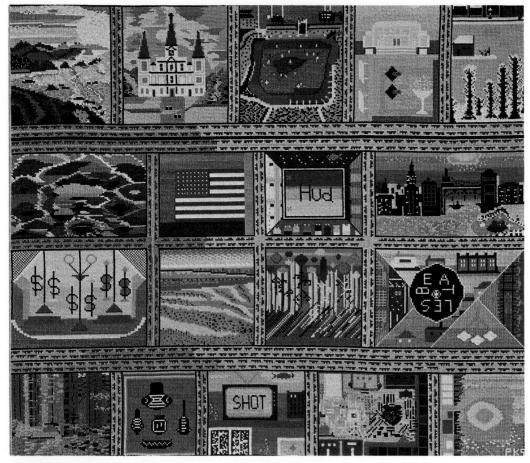

31. Pauline Shapiro, America 1963. Collection Mrs. Eleanor Steinman, New York.

32. Laura Lynch, View from Maggie's Window. Jay Johnson Gallery, New York.

Born in Iredell, a tiny village on the Bosque River halfway between Austin and Fort Worth, Aunt Clara's earliest memory was of her pioneer mother sewing hooked rugs and piecing quilts. She even remembered her mother's deciding that their spartan cottage needed a "picture"—and *painting* one, a first attempt Clara's father promptly framed.

But Clara's important childhood influences were the folk crafts, the gaily patterned quilts and rugs, and the spaciousness of the Texas landscape, which required some knowledge of perspective to be reduced to canvas size. In her earliest paintings she instinctively related objects in space from three different points of reference defined by diagonals. Moreover, in a painting such as *Arbor Meeting* (plate 20), as the Vogels point out, "Aunt Clara can tell us who each person is, and his whole life history," and this individuality with which she endowed her friends and neighbors of long ago makes them real for us today:

> The vitality and animation of the living is always in true contrast to the inanimate.... There is an implicit sense of air that is breathed in all her paintings, of air that can in a moment turn into a breeze to stir the branches of the trees, turn the windmill, riffle the hair of the people, moving through her canvases. Not only the animation of what is immediately occurring is communicated, but anticipation of what will happen next.

It was in 1945 that Clara Williamson began to paint. She had always wanted to, but the obligations of taking care of an older husband and raising a son had to be met first. She had already moved to Dallas. She started sketching, drawing on her prodigious visual memory of the past. Enrolling in a class at Southern Methodist University, where she amused but soon awed the young students who gave her her nickname, she learned enough elementary perspective to paint her first memory picture. *Chicken for Dinner* won the first of many awards. "I succeed," she said later, "at least in the truthfulness of the subject though not in any degree of perfection of execution. I have never yet made a painting that measured up to my mental picture." The homily had been put in almost the same words 150 years before by the greatest of all creators: "The true artist has no pride . . . he has a vague awareness of how far he is from reaching his goal; and while others may perhaps be admiring him, he laments the fact that he has not yet reached the point whither his better genius only lights the way for him like a distant sun."

Donald Vogel, watching Clara Williamson painting away at her easel in the back of the art class (fig. 71B), absorbing all the information she needed but oblivious to all the highfalutin' art jargon, asked her why she painted from top to bottom as though lowering a windowshade. "To keep my hands from getting in the paint," she answered. How vividly I recalled, reading this, Rigaud Benoit's response from up on the scaffold of Ste. Trinité Cathedral (see pp. 121–23) one day in 1949 when I asked him why he was painting a tiny drainpipe invisible from the nave—"to keep the thatch from rotting"—and how this response made me realize for the first time that for the popular artist there are no aesthetic problems, only practical ones.

71B. Clara McDonald Williamson, Street-Car
at Waxachie. Courtesy Kevin E. Vogel.

72. Clara McDonald Williamson, White Sands,
New Mexico, Sunset. Collection the author.

Summing up what it is that constitutes Clara Williamson's distinction, what places her outside the ranks of the quaint and charming and in the company of such masters as Hicks and Bombois, Pippin and Kane, Vogel concludes that it is the great "generosity" of the popular masters "that they share their inner life, their personal essences with us. They paint from the heart. . . . There is no gradual evolution of style . . . air surrounds the objects: the clean, clear soft light that enables one to see objects sharply defined at great distances (fig. 72).

Frank Baldwin (1878–1964)

There are instances in Haiti and Brazil where an unknown artist, sometimes even a nameless one, paints a half-dozen superb pictures, or perhaps only one, and then vanishes. The first of such artists in America was Joseph Pickett (1848–1918), a lower-middle-class carnival handyman of New Hope, Pennsylvania, who worked for years on four serene, beautifully painted landscapes, and whose wife put the seal on his total isolation as an artist when she remarked derisively to a neighbor, "If Joe wants to paint and does not get paint on the carpet, it's all right with me."

Such an artist existed in our time in the little town of Pittsburgh, New Hampshire, close to the Canadian border. All we know about him is that his name was Frank Baldwin, that he spent most of his adult years buying up the town's businesses, from lumber to groceries, and that later on in life he became a recluse, a religious mystic, and took to painting. But whether the *Crucifixion* (plate 21), was one of a kind, or one of several now lost forever, will probably never be known. It was bought in a garage sale after the artist's death and almost thrown away before Baldwin's discoverer, David Wiggins, traced it to New York and brought it back to New Hampshire.

One could say that Frank Baldwin had seen examples of early Renaissance painting before embarking on his *Crucifixion*. The composi-

73. Frank Baldwin, Crucifixion *(detail). Courtesy David Wiggins.*

tion is familiar. But what he has done with the figures, the land-scape—and that sky!—is unprecedented. Perhaps his preoccupation with the grain of the wood, a preoccupation that carries over into the grainy stones and robes as well, may be attributed to his familiarity with the freshly minted products of his sawmill (figs. 73, 74). Perhaps the distant hills are reminiscent of the White Mountains at sundown. But the intensity with which grief and anger are rendered; the art with which the figures are deployed and then locked into place, and the fluidity of that sky which seems to mourn with the mourners could only have been painted by a mystic who had become—if only this once—a true artist (fig. 75).

Among the suggestive details told me by Mr. Wiggins was this one. The original frame of the *Crucifixion* had been hand-carved and had handles. How fitting, and touching, that the artist envisioned his masterpiece being carried through the streets as in a medieval procession or a South American religious festival!

74. Frank Baldwin, Crucifixion *(detail). Courtesy David Wiggins.*

75. Frank Baldwin, Crucifixion *(detail). Courtesy David Wiggins.*

76. William Edmondson, Jezebel. Collection Edmund Fuller.

4
Artists of the Black Experience

76. William Edmondson, Jezebel. Collection Edmund Fuller.

William Edmondson (c.1883–1951): Miracles I Can Do

Dis here stone 'n all those out there in de yard come from God. It's de word in Jesus speakin' his mind in my mind, I must be one of his 'ciples. These here is mirkels I can do. Can't nobody do these but me. I can't help carvin'. I jes does it. It's like when you're leavin' here you goin' home.
—WILLIAM EDMONDSON *quoted in* Time,
1 November 1937

THE RECORDS of his birth and death were lost in fires. The site of his grave is not known. Up to 1907 he worked in the repair shops of the Nashville, Chattanooga & St. Louis Railway. Injured and in a cast for months, he next worked in Nashville's all-white Baptist Hospital as servant, foreman, janitor, orderly. Since his parents had been slaves, he had an exhilarating sense of freedom. "I

77. *William Edmondson, birdbath.*

78. *William Edmondson, Angel. Collection the author.*

79. *William Edmondson, Eve.*

worked when I felt like it." One day, probably in 1931, when he was more than fifty, he began "hacking away at stones." People laughed but he was not discouraged: "I had a vision." Chipping away at discards from lintels and curbstones, limestone mostly, he began to make tombstones for $2 apiece or a bottle of gin. What was that vision? "God spoke to me from the head of the bed like a natural man. He talked so loud he woke me. He told me to pick up tools and go to work. . . . He told me to cut the figures." The tools were a hammer, a file, and two "chisels" made from iron spikes. The massive neckless figures began to emerge as if they had always been there, just as he saw them (fig. 76). "I cut stingily," he said. The whites in their segregated cemeteries wanted no part of these "stingily hewn" angels and birds. "It ain't got much style," he mused. "God don't want much style." But wealthy neighbors, Alfred and Elizabeth Starr, and their friend Sidney Hirsch, were amazed by what they saw. They bought figures and commissioned birdbaths (fig. 77). The photographers Edward Weston and Louise Dahl-Wolfe came to take pictures. Publisher William Randolph Hearst wouldn't let Dahl-Wolfe's portraits of a black man appear in *Harper's Bazaar,* so the photographer took them to the Museum of Modern Art where on October 27, 1937, Alfred Barr, one of the early enthusiasts of popular art, exhibited twelve of the sculptures. There was no catalogue, there were no sales, and soon the very name of the artist faded from memory.

My own included—but not my memory of what I had seen. In 1956, on my first visit to Nashville, I made inquiries. The artist's name was William Edmondson but he had died, alas, in 1951. I talked to the Starrs and all the other "society folk" who had collected his work in

78.   79.

80. William Edmondson, Crucifixion. *Abby Aldrich Rockefeller Collection.*

the early days. They recalled that the old man had been enough impressed by his New York exposure to double his prices from $2 to $4—if his clients could afford it, Edmondson had added. They admitted ruefully that they'd neglected him in the last decade of his life. Many of the great pieces were now standing in gardens, overgrown with shrubs, the soft stone crumbling under rain and snow. I took an *Angel* (fig. 78) home with me to New Jersey, discovering years later how it had looked when freshly carved—in a photo of the great man standing in his "quarry," leather-aproned, smiling quizzically. There he had stood surrounded by an assortment of birds, birdbaths, prizefighters, biblical figures, "uplifted ladies," Crucifixions, critters and varmints—not to mention Eleanor Roosevelt (twice), *The Dietitian of McGannon Hall,* a planter in the shape of a coffee pot, and my stone angel, beady-eyed and inscrutable.

It would be a presumption to attempt to explain how Edmondson did what he did. No precedents, no rules, no aesthetic inhibitions stood in his way (fig. 79). He speaks for himself inimitably. "I looked up in the sky and right there in the noon daylight He hung a tombstone out for me to make." In the last year of his life, almost blind but still carving, he depended on youngsters to lift the heavier pieces into trucks. "Don' drop that stone, honey, it's paid fo'."

Horace Pippin (1888–1946)

Pictures just come to my mind and then I tell my heart to go ahead.

—HORACE PIPPIN

Horace Pippin's discovery, by the Pennsylvania art critic Christian Brinton and the famous illustrator N. C. Wyeth, came in the forty-ninth year of his life when he had only just begun to paint. In the nine years that were left to him, Pippin painted all but one of his important pictures, was exhibited (with Kane and others) at the Museum of Modern Art, was given half a dozen one-man shows, was collected greedily by connoisseurs in the Philadelphia and New York areas, and enjoyed considerable fame.

Long before it was acknowledged that "Black is beautiful" and that Afro-Americans had created a culture of their own in the United States, Horace Pippin had unselfconsciously celebrated these self-evident truths in his paintings—unselfconsciously because in the time and circumstances in which he lived, only a handful of intellectuals had formulated such concepts. Pippin's pride in being black is manifest in all his works (fig. 81). And in many of his best pictures his pride in being a part of his race's heroic struggle out of slavery and toward self-fulfillment is just as manifest.

Was Horace Pippin a "great painter" in the accepted canon of Western art, or only a "talented primitive"? This is a question as meaningless as comparing apples and eggplants. Masters of popular art, by their intuitive grasp of the principles of composition, color, and accommodation to the flatness of the picture plane achieve the same effect of timelessness as the recognized masters. There is the same sense of arrested mobility, the same transformation of the humble into the noble, the here-and-now into forever. In academic painting, which busies itself with surface resemblances, this never happens. Content (the subject, the message) is not deeply felt; and therefore one is conscious only of the artist's skill. But the Brueghels and the Pippins have

81. Horace Pippin, Asleep. Museum of Art, Carnegie Institute.

this in common: everything is subordinated to the unfolding vision, the creation of a world.

Instinctively Pippin worked from the world he knew: the world of nature, the world of Goshen and his mother's memories, the world of West Chester, the world of impoverished, hardworking, hard-fighting, suffering, and enduring blacks. It was a world that needed no ideology to make it real, no prettifying to make it palatable.

In such great pictures as *Domino Players* (plate 22), *Amish Letter Writer* (fig. 82), *The Barracks,* (plate 23), *The Park Bench,* the *John Brown* trio, the *Holy Mountain* quartet, and the final glowing flower pieces (fig. 83), Pippin bequeathed a world to his people—and to mankind.

83. Horace Pippin, Flowers with Hat and Cane. Collection Walter Lyons.

84. *Horace Pippin,* John Brown Going to His Hanging. *Pennsylvania Academy of Arts.*

85. *Horace Pippin,* John Brown Reading His Bible. *Andrew Crispo Gallery, New York.*

He was born on February 22, 1888, in West Chester, Pennsylvania, just twenty-five years after the Civil War and less than twenty miles from the South. His grandparents had been slaves and his grandmother had witnessed the hanging of John Brown, the white abolitionist whose attack on the federal arsenal at Harpers Ferry had touched off the great conflict. Years later Pippin would paint three of his best pictures about this legendary hero of his childhood. The first and greatest of them, *John Brown Going to His Hanging* (fig. 84), shows the scene his mother so often described.

John Brown Reading His Bible (fig. 85) carries more emotional weight than the other two. Perhaps this is because it is so lacking in ac-

tion, so bare and quiet, yet filled with such a foreboding tension. Again, the scene is authentic.... Brown had started life as a free-thinker but soon returned to the Calvinist faith of his father, reading his Bible, his biographers say, "with single-minded determination." This was the Brown that Pippin portrayed in a log cabin resembling a jail cell, reading at night by candlelight. This was the Brown who memorized the doomsday prophecies of Isaiah and Jeremiah—"And I will feed them that oppress thee with their own flesh; and they shall be drunken with their own blood"—Brown the accuser, implacable, unforgiving.

In 1911 Horace Pippin's mother died, and he wasted no time in leaving his job in Goshen, New York, and moved to Paterson, New Jersey. He was at Mahwah, up the Ramapo River, working for the American Brakeshoe Company when the United States became involved in World War I and he enlisted.

Pippin's first paintings were to come out of the vivid memory of what followed, but he waited until the last year of his life to sum up what he had gone through. He must have put *The Barracks* off so long because he sensed that it would require his full powers to describe inaction without being boring about it. The scene could double for the trenches. The soldiers in their improvised underground bunks are passing the time—sleeping, mending clothes, writing letters—as isolated from one another as though in solitary confinement.

As always with great painters, the message is conveyed by pictorial means: in this case the horizontals and verticals from which there is no escape; the depressing gradations of grays and browns suggesting death; the murky candlelight providing just enough illumination of such significant details as the black hand on the white pad, the guns and gas masks, the muddy floor. During those days and months in the trenches Pippin had constantly written in his diary and made sketches. He was fascinated with both the factual horrors of war and the beauty of the French countryside. But as he moved forward from battle to battle with the heroic (all-black) Fifteenth New York Regiment, most of these drawings had to be discarded and were lost forever.

Those that survive reveal what the diary conceals. The war had been a shattering experience to Horace Pippin. He would not have admitted it. He may not even have known it. But the drawings, and to a greater degree the paintings that grew out of them, are evidence that cannot be denied. He had seen the desolation of the earth, the ruin of cities, the inhumanity of man. The Bible said that all men were brothers, and Pippin believed this as firmly as he believed anything. Then what was the meaning of this Thing they had sent him into, this suffering and killing? He could not say. There could be only one way to get at the truth. But his right arm, the only instrument he had to release what was fighting inside him, had been paralyzed by a sniper's bullet. He invented an artist's therapy to limber it up: engraving pictures on old cigar-box tops with a red-hot poker. *The Getaway* (fig. 86) is one of the pictures of this time of adjustment that reflects his loneliness.

All that changed when Pippin's first show opened at the Carlen

86. Horace Pippin, The Getaway. Collection Mrs. Edmund C. Evans and Miss Ellen Winsor.

Gallery in January 1940. It was an instant success. The artist, reading the reviews and noting the sales, smiled broadly. "The boys are doin' me good," he said. One of the "boys" was Albert C. Barnes of the Barnes Foundation, who bought six of the pictures and wrote a note for the catalogue comparing Pippin to Kane. But Barnes's ill-advised attempt to "educate" Pippin in one of the classes for "advanced" artists at the Foundation ended when the great artist went to sleep, snoring loudly.

How the white man's well-stuffed drawing rooms must have looked to the furtive gaze of the "colored laundress's son" is reflected

87. Horace Pippin, The Den. Collection Mrs. Arnold Gingrich.

88. Horace Pippin, Holy Mountain No. 2. Private collection.

in the Victorian Interiors, as Carlen called them. One such was *The Den,* painted for Jane Hamilton as a "surprise" following an afternoon in her Paoli manor house during which the artist absorbed many drinks but forgot nothing (fig. 87). The one that finally wound up in New York's Metropolitan Museum has the same magical, stupendously balanced presence.

In December 1941, when the United States was plunged into the Second World War, Pippin, who had experienced the horrors of the First, could not face another holocaust without some hope for the future, and the *Holy Mountain* series was that affirmation (fig. 88). "If a man knows nothing but hard times," he had written, "he will paint them, for he must be true to himself, but even that man may have a dream and the 'Holy Mountains' are my answer to such dreaming." He was working on the fifth of the series, a blasted tree in front of a bare mountain split by an ugly fissure, when his heart stopped. It was July 6, 1946.

The Two Minnies

Many black American artists in the three decades since Pippin's death have contributed to the imagery of their people's experience. Some, like Jacob Lawrence and Romare Bearden, have been highly sophisticated. Others, like Elijah Pierce, the Cleveland barber who carves and polychromes figures that tell a story, are deservedly popular.

I have chosen two relatively unknown painters to conclude this chapter. Both are southern ladies. The black Minnie (Evans (1892–)

paints white people predominantly (plate 28). The white Minnie (Deschamps) (1907–) paints blacks only (plate 27). There is not a trace of *hubris* in either artist. Yet surely this reversal of expected subjects springs from the inequality of life in the South. (Life is as unequal in the North, but for different reasons.) Minnie Evans's years spent as a domestic among enlightened, art-conscious whites no doubt gives the gods and angels of her dreams their light complexions. Minnie Deschamps, almost as unconsciously, recognizes the greater vitality and rootedness of the sharecroppers, a world she could never enter except through her pictures. The important word in both cases is "unconscious," for too much consciousness of intention in an artist leads to self-consciousness, willful attempts to please (or defy) one's audience, images that instead of coming naturally, spring only from the top of the mind.

Minnie Evans's visions—unindividualized, symmetrical, vaguely symbolic, surrealist (fig. 89)—have been compared to those of the "apocalyptic" Blake, but there is none of Blake's classical draftsmanship, social conscience, or profoundly poetic "minute particulars." The comparison is helpful only to the extent that both artists are trustful of impulse and are inspired by the Book of Revelations. It has been speculated that the nature in Minnie Evans's paintings reflects the twenty-seven years she spent taking admissions at Airlie Gardens in Wil-

89. Minnie Evans, Solomon's Temple. Jay Johnson Gallery, New York.

90. *Minnie Deschamps,* On the Fence. *Collection the author.*

mington, North Carolina, but her flowering shrubs are not that specific.

The paintings of Minnie Deschamps are at once more conventional and more subtle. Rural South Carolina has changed even less since plantation times than has the North Carolina of Minnie Evans's childhood, and it is the poetry of this rural "timeless" existence among the poor blacks that Minnie Deschamps captures so poignantly. Self-taught, self-assured, extroverted, this artist paints in a casein emulsion sometimes mixed with ink on the rough side of marilla paper and frames her pictures in double narrow wooden strips separated by wide bands of burlap. Had she seen the photos of Walker Evans and Dorothea Lange? the paintings of Ben Shahn or Robert Gwathmey? Their accuracy of attitudes is there, the candid-camera compositional "fix," but there is no trace of caricature or irony in Minnie Deschamps's art, much less anger or pity. This is the way the world is: take it or leave it (fig. 90). Secure in her way of life—she runs three farms, raising cotton, corn, soybeans, wheat, tomatoes, and several thousand chickens, not to mention participation in tournament golf—Minnie Deschamps is too much a part of her local community to regard the rich with envy or the poor with guilt.

I called her once at her home in Sumter, South Carolina, to ask her why she painted only her black neighbors. "A friend asked me that years ago," she laughed. "I'd never thought about it! So I painted a picture of my white neighbors. When my friend saw it, she threw up her hands and covered her eyes. 'I was wrong, Minnie,' she said. 'Stick to what turns you on. Stick to what you love.'"

91. *Facade of sign shop of Joseph Joseph, Buffalo (1883).*

PERHAPS ARTISTS HAD always done it and nobody noticed. Or perhaps it was done by the anonymous carvers of the church portals, or the artists of the early Renaissance like Ambrogio Lorenzetti and Benozzo Gozzoli, bemused by pageantry, by mankind *en masse*. But something new was introduced in twentieth-century America: the knowledge that there was no longer any place for such artists in a culture split between the intellectualism of the avant-garde and the crass materialism that appealed to the lower, middle, and working classes. And along with this desperate sense of isolation came a deep resentment (most often unconscious) that this should be so, and this resentment was reflected in the materials used: junk, throwaways, everything vulgar and disposable that could nevertheless be sublimated by sheer quantity and the dispositions of an artist's soul into art inself.

Long before the avant-garde discovered that junk labeled "art" could be sold at a profit, long before Stankiewicz welded pipes to rusted antennae, Chamberlin put smashed cars on pedestals, or Warhol made Campbell's soup cans and Brillo boxes into assemblies mocking their intended uses, Simon Radilla of Watts had buried his Hudson touring car in the backyard and begun to erect his towering monument out of welded pipe, Coca-Cola bottles, and bowling balls.

But Radilla was not the first. Some "assemblages," like Joseph Joseph's multipainted shop front in Buffalo (fig. 91), date back into the nineteenth century. Some, like the portrait of a nagging wife slyly carved into the rump of a carousel horse by its maker, are as old as traveling circuses. Some of the artists are specialists, like the tattoo technicians within a profession that reaches as far as the jungles of the Amazon, where body painters still create designs of great beauty. "I've made more lasting impressions on people than any other artist," quipped "Spider" Webb (fig. 92). A tattooed Scythian chieftain was found frozen and perfectly preserved in a Russian tomb dating back to 2500 B.C. The Egyptians practiced the art with their usual elegance and

5
Artists of the Total Environment

92. Tattooed lady. Courtesy Fred and Mary Fried.

93. *Mural on parking lot wall, Los Angeles (1971).*

so did American Indians, until the missionaries, those traditional enemies of art, threatened them with Leviticus 19:28 ("Ye shall not make any cuttings in your flesh for the dead, nor print any marks upon ye.") And in 1971 the Los Angeles Fine Arts Squad painted on a parking lot's concrete wall a frightening vision of what to expect if the environmentalists have their wings clipped by big-business government (fig. 93)—another example of environmental art.

Fred and Mary Fried researched such arts, from the banner painters who followed in the wake of Hogarth and Hicks to the carvers of lovers' initials on trysting trees, and their latter-day heirs from "Kilroy" in World War II to the desperate graffiti-artists who turn the subway cars of New York into scabrous horrors compatible with the other components in that hell of mass transit. The common ground in all these arts which seem to serve as whipping boys for man's frustrations and prejudices is summarized by the Frieds: "There is art that was shot at, thrown at, slung at, and laughed at. There is people's art that struck back at their oppressors. And there is accidental art, made because it cried out for being, captured in a tree trunk or in a group of found objects."

The Artist Nobody Knew

Such a one, so supreme in his isolation that even his name has never been established, was Simon (or Sam) Radilla (or Rodia) (1898–). I sought him out and interviewed him in the early fifties; but a decade later he had lost hope, abandoned his unwanted and threatened masterpiece, and gone off to die in an anonymity as complete as that which had shrouded his mysterious appearance.

Watts, the black district of Los Angeles where Radilla bought his pie-shaped lot around 1920, lies in a no-man's land of deteriorating bungalows that stretches interminably through the featureless flats between Pasadena, the upper-middle-class Nirvana, and Long Beach,

94. Simon Radilla, Watts Towers, Los Angeles (1951).

95. Simon Radilla at Watts (1951).

the end of the road from Iowa which has been called a cemetery with lights.

Crossing the railroad tracks, the towers loom suddenly (fig. 94). Radilla wanted it that way. He wanted the towers to be seen. A hill would have been better, but the hills of Los Angeles had already been spoken for. At least from these tracks the towers would be visible from the trains. But who rides in trains any more, least of all through downtown Los Angeles? Should a citizen stung by a spirit of adventure get as far as Watts, the chances are he would not see the towers at all. Though the tallest is 104 feet, they are not conspicuous from five blocks off and at ten, dwarfed by high-tension pylons and radio transmitters, they are invisible.

Created entirely out of junk, this strange, abstractly beautiful work of art was still growing when I visited it. In fact, Simon Radilla, attached by his window-cleaner's belt to the webbing like a benevolent spider, was adding a new series of flying buttresses—7-Up bottles with their orange labels facing out—the day I visited him. This tower had been only twenty-five feet high in 1922. A fresh set of necklaces brought it up to thirty, and so on. After the metal rods and mesh and a mixture of waterproof cement came the artifacts of our civilization: orange squeezers, bottle caps, willowware, percolators, hair setters, telephone insulators, burnt-out bulbs, tooth mugs, pieces of old mirrors, a glass shoe, a three-finger bowling ball. There was no conscious choice of objects just as there was no deliberate plan in their arrangement. The objects were whatever was discarded, available in quantity, and resistant to time and tremor. The design is always mysteriously incomplete. Seventy-five thousand seashells embedded in the stern of this triangular ironclad would be overpowering if arranged symmetrically. As they are, in half circles and broken spokes of low relief, the effect is something like the awesome confusion of stars in the Milky Way. Only slightly more conventional are the volutes and cake stamps stenciled into the pavement, the concave "fossils" of Simon's hammer, compass, and chisel in a lunette of the side wall (fig. 96), the rhythmic corncobs and stalks of wheat like emblems of fertility above the foun-

96. Radilla's imprinted tools (detail).

tains. These, too, are removed from the commonplace by being always sprained a little off their centers. Most astonishing is the seemingly unerring taste with which fragmented tiles of a thousand varieties are related in color-key and flow of design around the basins and stalagmite-like lesser outcroppings.

The walls around the towers were not part of Simon's plan. For all the obscurity in which the towers grew, his will to communicate, to make their beauty available to everyone, was as strong then as it ever was. But the local police saw a hazardous temptation to climbing children, so the walls were built.

Simon Radilla was born in Italy in 1898, emigrating to the United States nine years later. Discharged from the Army Engineers in 1918 after serving in France, he resolved to begin work at once on his contribution to peace. "Why so many people want to shed blood?" he asked me. "You go to boxing match. It's when the nose is broken and blood flow over the boxer's eyes that people clap for joy. That's why, my dear friend, I not turn on this radio my niece give me." Simon preferred to play ancient Martinelli and Caruso records on the horn-phonograph that is the only piece of furniture besides the bed in his one-room shack behind the towers. Every cent he has made for thirty years, after paying for food and taxes, has gone into his masterwork. In the early days he set tiles and bought junk; then he worked off and on for the telephone company, crawling through their underground conduits to plug overhead leaks with handfuls of wet plaster. Soon the junk dealers were giving him their broken bottles and tiles, so that all his money went for the steel rods and wire mesh to make the towers earthquake- and bomb-proof. He expected them to be a beacon of hope when the materialistic parts of the city have met the fate they deserve . . .

Whether Cambodia or any other exotic culture entered into Radilla's calculations is as doubtful as the likelihood that he ever heard of the word "abstraction." That he saw San Marco or Monreale or Pompeii or the basilicas of Ravenna as a child is possible but not likely. All theorizings he answered with the simplicity of the true artist: "I had in my mind to do something big and I did it." Was there a religious inspiration? "I believe in God, dear friend," he said, "but Christ he not crucified to build the power of the wealthy Church. That why I take down many years ago cross that was on highest tower there. Why? Because priest come and rub hands; he think cross justify *him!*"

97. Watts Towers (detail).

The deep furrows in Simon's leathery skin contracted and he scratched his graying hair when asked to supply logical connections between some of his statements. This bewilderment, and the obvious relish with which he described the torments of Bruno and St. Simeon and identified himself with their martyrdom, raised questions about his sanity. To the average man, anyone who built the towers would have to be crazy.

"If he had not been a great fool," said Macauley of Boswell, "he would never have been a great writer." And the Italian painter Veronese, when hauled before the Inquisition and ordered to substitute the Magdalene for a dog in one of his frescoes, refused with the words: "We artists take the same liberties as poets and madmen." The knowing artist in our time is inevitably the victim of his intelligence and his conscience. His conscience drives him in the opposite direction from the "poet and madman," making him deny pure fantasy as the most cowardly escape from social responsibility, while his torturing intelligence constantly reminds him that no rational protest can possibly counter the degradation of the norm. Simon Radilla, unlike Veronese, was not conscious of taking "liberties" since intuition was his only demon and censor. His gigantic protest against the megalopolis which epitomizes our materialism is effective precisely because it has no possible use.

James Hampton's *Throne of the Third Heaven*

While Louise Nevelson was making it big in the establishment art world with her "inscrutable" assemblages of wooden junk-boxes painted black, James Hampton was building his own total environment as compulsively (plate 26, fig. 98). Not for art's sake but for religion's—Hampton's own religion. And not for an orbit into the rarefied purlieus of intellectual art critics and millionaire collectors, but for all

the people, he hoped. But this impossible dream grew and grew, like all the visions of the mystics, privately; so privately that it was discovered only after the artist had died—and then only by an ironic accident. The rent on the garage where Hampton had been secreting his magic was no longer being paid, and just as all this "junk" was about to be swept away by the angry landlord, the perceptive Smithsonian Institution stepped in and paid the back rent. Thus was the *Third Heaven* saved forever—or for as long as the first and second worlds with their heavens survive.

Like Simon Radilla, Hampton was one of modern society's moles—but in this instance a Kafkaesque mole of the lower middle class, lost in the tunnels of the bureaucracy, choking on the printouts of the computers, a robot among robots who would never have guessed what their square brother was doing and would surely have laughed derisively had they known. It's almost too perfect that this magnificently bizarre work originated in Washington, D.C., and that in Washington it's to be seen today (fig. 99). It could only have been created by a recluse. All the compulsive total-environmentalists were reclusive: Simon Radilla, as we have seen; Creek Charlie, painting polka dots on houses, trees, even the clothes he wore in his shack in the southwest corner of Virginia; Walter Flax, the genial black naval buff who assembled a whole fleet of make-believe ironclads in a vacant lot behind the Yorktown Memorial; Sister Gertrude Morgan, the New Orleans gospel singer who painted in wax crayons—on lampshades, toilet paper, and the plastic supermarket trays used for packaging frozen meats—her visions of soaring (*Jesus Is My Airplane*) with a red-haired groom over the New Jerusalem.

Hampton (1909–1964) called his creation *The Throne of the Third Heaven of the Nations Millennium General Assembly* and on a bulletin board in the garage on Seventh Street N.W., he tacked this injunction from Proverbs 29:18: "Where there is no vision the people perish." In two written commentaries on his work (one in cabalistic cipher still

98. *James Hampton with his* Throne of the Third Heaven. *Smithsonian Institution.*

99. *James Hampton,* Throne of the Third Heaven. *Smithsonian Institution.*

100. James Hampton, Throne of the Third Heaven *(detail). Smithsonian Institution.*

defies the cryptographers), he referred to himself in governmentese as "St. James, Director of Special Projects for the State of Eternity." Wittily, and to the point, Elinor Lander Horwitz comments: "Perhaps he smiled at the bureaucratic title, but then again, perhaps he did not." There is no trace of humor on the artist's face as he stands for the photograph—balding, bespectacled, conventionally garbed even to the triangle of handkerchief peeping from his top left pocket. When not actually at work inside the garage, he'd sit outside facing a table with some nails and glue, giving nickels and dimes to winos who'd bring him tinfoil or discarded furniture, while he moulded wings and crowns or sheathed light bulbs and jelly jars in gold foil. After he died of cancer, a friend who owned a nearby clothing store speculated about the artist's intentions. Did all the excess space in the garage indicate that Hampton would have established his own church there, with seats in the foreground, himself preaching from the throne? It seems unlikely. Like Nevelson's and the work of other artist-mystics, it speaks for itself (fig. 100).

Pauline Shapiro (1915–1972) and Laura Lynch (1949–)

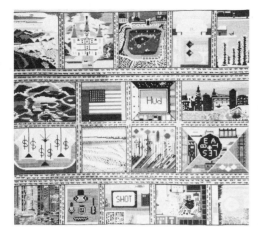

101. *Pauline Shapiro,* America 1963. *Cotton needlepoint on canvas. Collection Eleanor Steinman.*

The folk needlework of colonial New England and Pennsylvania had no immediate issue. But the memory of all that *fractur* calligraphy and those "Home, Sweet Home" pillows lingered on. The great tapestries of medieval and Renaissance Europe were widely reproduced and many were hung in American museums. But how this coalesced in the wholly original "quilt" of a Queens, Long Island, recluse is one of those enigmas that make art forever mysterious. Surely the still-frames of cinema were part of the late Pauline Shapiro's inspiration; perhaps even more immediately the newspaper reproductions of the famous Zapruder home movie that inadvertently caught the tragic assassination of President Kennedy, which figures in the sixteenth unit of *America 1963* and gives it its ironic undertones (plate 31, fig. 101). The medium of the 39″ × 46″ picture was needlepoint; the thread cotton of the best quality. None of Pauline Shapiro's works were sketched in advance or even drawn on the canvas; and none were ever offered for sale.

Less symbol-laden but wonderfully evocative of urban life is Laura Lynch's *The View from Maggie's Window.* Here, self-illuminated, with a disco on the roof, is a glimpse into every aspect of *la vie quotidienne*—a voyeur's delight complete with field glasses; (plate 32). Laura Lynch puts her pictures together by appliquéing bits of felt and corduroy and then embroidering for fine details (fig. 102). The method had already been used effectively by Louise Berg Thiessen of Omaha, Nebraska, who sewed together strips cut from hat-bodies into landscapes of bewitching charm.

102. *Laura Lynch,* The View from Maggie's Window. *Jay Johnson Gallery, New York.*

6

Through Immigrants' Eyes

103. Morris Hirshfield, Self-Portrait. *Sidney Janis Gallery, New York.*

Morris Hirshfield (1872–1946)

UNCLASSIFIABLE, unprecedented, unconventional in every way—and having nothing in common with each other though they came from the same city—are the two urban immigrants who round out our survey of popular art in the United States. Much has been written about both painters. In Hirshfield's case the treatment has been so definitive and uncommonly astute as to make anything but a summary of appreciation redundant. The art critic–dealer Sidney Janis not only helped discover Hirshfield, retaining possession of all the pictures after the artist's ten-year career ended with his death in 1946, but has more than adequately analyzed the major pictures (see bibliography).

Repeating the pattern of so many of the world's outstanding popular artists, Hirshfield began to paint in his late sixties and with no technical preparation at all. A successful slipper manufacturer forced into retirement for reasons of health, he constructed his pictures of persons and places entirely with his inner eye. The visions derive in part from the ornate products of his trade. Children's picture books of "cute" animals (fig. 104) and childhood recollections of the Jewish and Russian Orthodox rituals under the czars (fig. 105) pretty much rounded out Hirshfield's memory bank.

Like Henri Rousseau, the French popular painter patronized by Apollinaire and Picasso, Hirshfield painted a world of bizarre beasts and sexy women (fig. 106) with so much repressed passion and so little knowledge of the conventions of art that nothing he ever created could be mistaken for the work of any other artist (plate 25). So great, in fact, was this artist's conviction of the reality of what he painted that the viewer simply accepts it. Cats, jungle or domestic, seem to be wearing fur coats. Boudoir slippers (naturally) are more important than diamonds. Men and beasts with tiny extremities, nudes with weird torsos, sleigh-rides over snow like cotton balls or asbestos (fig. 107), water that ripples like well-brushed mohair—all provide the anatomy of Hirshfield's wonderfully consistent world.

Girl in a Mirror (plate 24) depicts the artist's shy vision of feminine seductiveness before he had acquired the temerity to confront his dream-girls head on. Note that the reflected image is impossibly twisted in order to conceal the erogenous zones. But consciously or not, Hirshfield used the fuzzy pyramidal tip of the potted plant to double as his model's pubic hair. The reflection of the nude's left arm holding a powder puff would have overcomplicated the picture so the artist summarily eliminated it. Who cares? Certainly not the spectator, to whom the painting is perfect of its kind, complete as it stands.

Ralph Fasanella (1914–   )

Only one American painter was making pictures out of the same elements as Ralph Fasanella, the poet of the militant working class, the man *Life* calls "the most popular American folk artist working today." In his early work (1928–48), the late Ben Shahn was that man. Shahn's ideology paralleled the New Deal's but with Marxist undertones. Organized labor was the hero. The capitalists, the Church, the military, the late Senator Joseph McCarthy were the villains. Sacco, Vanzetti, Tom Mooney, and the Rosenbergs were the martyrs of a "second" American revolution. Strikes, the confrontation between the fascist and communist powers in Spain, protests against the (American) use of atomic power were the events that absorbed both artists. During those two decades in which Shahn, a painter trained in France, pursued these angels and demons, he became the darling of the Museum of Modern Art and enjoyed widespread popularity among the art critics and museums. But by the time Fasanella's work began to catch on in the early seventies, Shahn's work had fallen into disrepute.

Why was this so? What did these two artists have in common? And how did they differ? Shahn's impact faded in the last two decades

104.

105.

104. Morris Hirshfield, Elephant. Pencil drawing. Sidney Janis Gallery, New York.

105. Morris Hirshfield, Moses and Aaron. Sidney Janis Gallery, New York.

106. Morris Hirshfield, Tailor-Made Girl. Collection Mr. and Mrs. Sidney Janis.

107. Morris Hirshfield, Sleigh-Ride. Sidney
Janis Gallery, New York.

106.

107.

108. *Ben Shahn, oil study for Washington Social Security Building mural. Collection the author.*

of his career. The titles of his pictures paid lip service to the old gods—especially to those made sacred by the Soviet Union during the cold war and in its competition with the United States for nuclear power. But organized labor (the AFL–CIO) had long since lost its militancy, becoming an integral part of the capitalist system. And Shahn's visual symbols had by this time become too abstract to reach anyone but the intellectuals. The intellectuals' art critics, by now committed to the uncompromising "purity" of abstract expressionism, derisively rejected Shahn's tightrope performance.

Shahn had never been a "popular artist" in the sense that Fasanella is, and that all the other artists discussed in this book are. He was not self-taught. He studied and imitated the French avant-garde until 1932, when with his Sacco-Vanzetti series, which established his reputation, he discarded the French baggage which conflicted with both his immigrant background and his new-found ideology, and began to acquire very skillfully many of the traits of the self-taught whose works he now admired (fig. 108). Pippin's paintings had their first New York sales in Shahn's gallery. And Shahn recognized such an affinity with the "cool" style of the Haitian Philomé Obin (see pp. 111–15) that he bought two of that popular master's pictures in Obin's first New York exhibit. Flat patterns, rejection of deep perspective, and intense concentration on the details of everyday life constituted the new style. Cheap clothes, old-fashioned shoes, hats of folded newsprint, backdrops of signboards and decaying dumbbell flats were echoes of Shahn's youth in Brooklyn, when the tough guys on his block, hearing that he had artistic talent, had put a piece of chalk in his hand, pointed to the sidewalk, and said, "OK, draw, you little bastard!"

Fasanella's childhood in the immigrant slums of New York was similar but the differences were significant. The family from southern Italy had none of the Old World respect for craftsmanship that Shahn's Ashkenazi parents brought with them from the ghetto in Lithuania. In the long run Fasanella profited greatly from not having either the time or the inclination to think of himself as an artist until his rebellion against the system was too ingrained to slough off; his style took much longer to develop but it owed nothing to exotic influences. Its cumulative power was based on observation and anger alone. Shahn romanticized the working class. Fasanella couldn't have if he'd wanted to. He was part of it. From the age of eight to fourteen, he had worked on his father's ice wagon twelve to fourteen hours a day "and every day I used to get a beating because I ran away." When that didn't work, his father gave up and sent him to the Catholic House of Correction in the Bronx—illegally, but in those days who cared?

"What did you learn there, Ralph?" I asked him.

"Certainly not religion!"

"No. But if you hadn't gone there, wouldn't you have joined the street gang like the other Italian kids, and maybe even the Mafia?"

"I guess. My father was always too tired to beat me hard. So he turned me over to the Fathers who *live* to beat up kids—if they can't *have* them, and I refused to be had. So they straightened me out, I guess, and I have to thank them for teaching me by their example that it's wrong for the big bullies to push the little guys around. I learned that life is unfair. So when I got out I was ready for labor politics, for the ideas of guys like Gene Debs and Scott Nearing, and later the Commies, who at least fought and died for something bigger than themselves."

After a stint in Spain fighting Franco in the Communist Abraham Lincoln Brigade, Fasanella came back, worked for Vito Marcantonio's American Labor Party, and ran for the City Council on the same ticket—more than enough to put him on the FBI's "red" list for good. He began organizing electrical workers around the country for $90 a month. "I had a knack. Few have it. I could go out now and bring in fifty new recruits in an hour if they took me to the gates. But when the unions became part of the very business system they were born to fight, they lost me. That was when I decided to take up painting."

That was in 1945. He began painting ten hours a day with the same committed fury he'd put into Spain, the street demonstrations, the recruiting at the gates. And—like all the great popular artists who started late in life—he painted his memories. These included his searing childhood, his bitterness over his father's wasted life—he appears as a crucified figure suspended by his own ice tongs in many of the son's pictures (fig. 109)—the churches nestling in fiery constriction between the tomblike office buildings and the banks, the glory of the left-wing idealism in the old days, the heroism of the working class before it fattened up on the bribes and cheap rewards it had once denounced.

109. Ralph Fasanella, Joe, the Iceman, No. 4. Courtesy Eve Fasanella and the artist.

110. Ralph Fasanella, subway sketch on copy of New York Times. Courtesy Eve Fasanella and the artist.

He knew he had to learn to draw, so in the subways, on the classified section of the morning newspaper he carried to work, he sketched the straphangers (fig. 110). In Spain he'd visited a museum or two and came away only with the notion that big pictures are big money. Now he acquired a different perspective altogether. "Something—maybe the arthritis in my fingers?—made me want to rub paper. I had the itch to create space." This was in his Grove Street apartment. "I thought I was a smart guy until I started painting. A painting is not an end, it's a beginning," he told Patrick Watson years later, "it begins like life." Like Shahn he escaped from an early marriage—both wives were named Tillie—and entered into a "kind of holy communion" with his pigments. His sister moved in with him and for a while supported him while he delved into his rich memories of Sullivan Street. Eve Lazorek, his second wife, assumed the life-support role of sister Tess. He read a book or two—Christopher Caudwell's Illusion and Reality, Hawthorne's The Scarlet Letter (whose symbol of guilt, the letter A, he would put to use later). His mind began to resonate with echoes of native American lore: the ecclesiastical preachments and the cheap stained

111. Ralph Fasanella, Church Interior with Stained Glass. *Courtesy Eve Fasanella and the artist.*

glass, heavily leaded, he'd stared at in the Catholic Protectory (fig. 111). He painted his first great picture (plate 29), the church like a coffin exploding with hellfires between tomblike, faceless banks.

It took Fasanella twenty-five years to produce one hundred and fifty canvases, and during the last ten years before his work caught on in the early seventies, he had to evade the FBI's blacklisting with the unions by pumping gas in the Bronx. It was a story by Arthur Miller, but the reverse of *Death of a Salesman*. The seven-foot-long paintings of that period are well described by Nicholas Pileggi in the article that brought Fasanella fame:

Building walls open to show interiors of dowdy, uninhabited living rooms ("Poor people never use their living rooms"). Kitchens filled with families and the jumbled pipes of slum plumbing, extension cords and cheap kitchen gadgets so familiar to the poor. Tables are set, family snapshots are on the walls, slogans and formal portraits of neighbors appear at the windows that line the streets. Policemen, ice wagons, bakeries, bars—the whole broad, colorful vitality of city life is caught in Fasanella's paintings. He has allowed us to peek into a period when the city's slums were filled with the parents of today's suburbanites.

And the irony of it all—not lost on Fasanella himself—is that he himself has now become a suburbanite! Success, a wife with a genius for systematic promotion of his now very expensive paintings, and perhaps the inertia of age which makes him rationalize the advantages for his work in all this space, privacy, efficiency, and comfort has given Ralph a sense of guilt not entirely disguised by a wry sense of humor. I kidded him about painting a baseball game (fig. 112) and he countered

112. Ralph Fasanella, Baseball: Night Game Practice. *Courtesy Eve Fasanella and the artist.*

that by telling me how he'd gone to Lowell, Massachusetts, a couple of years before "to save my sanity" by painting scenes from the great (and largely forgotten) textile strike of 1912. "Not because anybody needed it, but to remind myself of all that heroism."

I kept coming back to *Gray Day* (plate 30, fig. 113), painted in 1962 and filled with the clichés of the Communist left during the McCarthy era: Harvey Metuso, the stool pigeon; "Reds" in court or in their cellblock; the Rosenbergs being electrocuted for selling (or giving) atomic secrets to the USSR, framed in a gigantic "A" with the eagle of death

113. Ralph Fasanella, Gray Day. Courtesy Eve Fasanella and the artist.

114. Ralph Fasanella, Zingarella. Courtesy Eve Fasanella and the artist.

over it. I kept thinking how I despised this strident ideology—and how little that mattered. It was a great picture pulsing with the life and rhetoric of the time and charged with the artist's passion. It stood for "injustice" just as effectively as Goya's *Execution of 3 May 1808* fixes for all time the state's implacable brutality against a helpless citizenry. Nor does one have to side for or against the church or on either side of business to feel the ritualistic glow of religion and the crushing weight of materialism in *Wall Street.* No more than one has to love the city life in those swarming tenements to be moved by Fasanella's almost apocalyptic identification with the weblike vitality of New York.

"No one since Shahn—" I started to say.

"I loved those Sacco and Vanzetti things," Ralph said, "but after the war he lost me."

"He lost his anger," I said.

"He became too big a success. And I don't say that out of envy or bitterness. Shahn said only nice things about my work. I'd like to like all his paintings, but when he started fuckin' around with all those goddam symbols ... come off it man! Say what you mean! *Don't be afraid of being understood.* Who are you impressing? The Museum of Modern Art? The fairy art critics?"

"There's one painting here," I said, "that seems to make a statement about the fullness of life without preaching any kind of a sermon about the working class."

"You mean the one hanging behind me? It's my favorite too—*Zingarella!*" (fig. 114).

"What does that mean?"

"It's an Italian word for a woman with a lot of pizazz. It's a tribute to a woman on our block in Sullivan Street who had it all. I've placed her, as you see, in this suburban dead end—"

"To keep you alive, Ralph?"

"Maybe!"

III

Afro-America: Haiti and Brazil

115. Mardi-Gras celebrant, Colon, Panama (1965).

Afro-Americans from William Edmondson and Horace Pippin to Jacob Lawrence and Romare Beardon draw on their African heritage, but they are to an even greater extent products of the culture in which they were born, grew up, and became artists. This is equally true of black artists from the Caribbean—descendants of slaves from the same parts of West Africa as those who went to Haiti and Brazil—as well as artists from Mexico, Guatemala, Belize, Honduras, Costa Rica, Venezuela, Colombia, Ecuador, Guiana and Surinam.

1
Introduction

There are anthropologists who point to the distinctly African features of the monumental "Olmec" heads unearthed at La Venta on Mexico's Caribbean coast. But the fact remains that this heritage has had little or no effect on the development of Mexican styles, pre- or post-Columbian, all of which are distinctively "Mexican," regardless of whether Indian or Hispanic influences predominated. This is true as well of the dominant styles in the smaller nations to the south on the narrowing North American continent. Only along the Caribbean littoral of Panama are there traces of art with a distinctly "African" look (fig. 115). And the same holds for the most part for the black enclaves south of the isthmus, with the exception of Surinam, where the so-called Bush Negroes were sufficiently isolated from the Dutch to have retained traces of their African heritage in the decoration of their homes (fig. 116), but without as yet creating popular painting or sculpture out of that heritage.

As for the Caribbean islands other than Haiti, the cultures of Spain, France, and England have in their various ways effectively stifled the African heritage brought there by the slaves in the seventeenth and eighteenth centuries. Whatever traces of the rich European cultures the voyagers brought with them they left as playthings not to be shared with the "subhuman" slaves or their "childlike" descendants. The Spanish *conquistadores* are notorious for having brought with them from the Old World little but their authoritarian government and ecclesiastic architecture. "We have a two-party system," the classic Latin-American joke goes. "One party is in the palace; the other party is in jail." In Spanish Cuba, where the joke is still a reality, it is repeated in whispers. In Spanish Santo Domingo it was whispered so often during the thirty-year terror of Trujillo that whispering became a habit. In Spanish Puerto Rico, where there was always a measure of personal freedom and where today political freedom is complete, a way had to be found to join the Latin-American weeping wall. To be free was bad enough, but to be prosperous was treason. Puerto Ricans are still not sure who they are. The island's only folk art, the diminutive *santos* once carved by aged *jibaros,* are not considered worthy of mention in compilations of Hispanic religious sculpture.

What the French did to the culture of "their" islands, Martinique and Guadaloupe, must be seen to be believed. The fictions of independence and racial equality are the rhetoric of a new servitude. The Communist mayor of Fort-de-France lives in Paris. In return for their sugar and coconuts the islanders are obliged to import everything from milk to newspapers from metropolitan France. I remember being driven around the capital by an embittered cultural civil servant, find-

116. *Bush-Negro home near Paramaribo, Surinam.*

ing nothing of interest in the boutiques but Haitian painting, and saying to him: "You have an Avenue Victor Hugo but where is your Avenue Victor Hugues?" and his answer: "The French select our heroes for us." The Alsatian Victor Schoelcher liberated Martinique's slaves according to the French rules. "Josephine is one of their heroes, not ours. We are more than ever under their thumb—more so now than when we were a colony."

There are exceptions to the colonial syndrome, of course. Trinidad, most populous, prosperous, and racially mixed of the British colonies, came out of its colonial cocoon with more than its flags flying. The carnival costumes and masks of Port of Spain are a folk art drawing creatively on the traditions of Spain, Africa, and Asian India, and with a potential for popular art as yet unrealized. The lyrics of the calypsos are folk poetry at its most pungent. Nor is all the highly acclaimed literature of Trinidad written by embittered exiles like V. S. Naipaul; the poems and plays by the black poet Derek Walcott are as powerful as anything to come out of the English tradition since W. H. Auden and Robert Lowell.

There are exceptional popular artists, too, looked down upon in their own neo-colonial cultures, but with a measure of recognition abroad. Justo Sisana emerged in the post-Trujillo Dominican Republic when President Lyndon B. Johnson sent a Marine division there to try to impose order during the civil war between pro- and anti-Communist forces, and Sisana's first paintings depicted Dominican leftists firing machine guns at American planes from the strategic Duarte Bridge in Santo Domingo (fig. 117). His first patron, ironically, was Ellsworth Bunker, the American peacemaker. Sisana's landscapes at that time

118. Mallica Reynolds (Kapo, on the left, with tourist official) in Kingston, Jamaica (1966).

117. Justo Sisana, Defense of the Duarte Bridge, *1965.*

were wonderfully free-floating, his trees like sea anemones, his clouds like cream puffs.

Equally original and more varied has been the painting of Mallica Reynolds (Kapo) in Kingston, Jamaica (fig. 118). A preacher of the Protestant Pocomania cult, Kapo's pictures range widely from religious visions and Biblical homilies to bathing beauties and personal anecdotes (fig. 119).

119. Kapo, Reconciliation. Collection the author.

2
Haiti

HAITIAN POPULAR ART—like its blood brothers in Yugoslavia, Brazil, and a very few other "underdeveloped" countries with rich folkish cultures—can properly be described by no other name. Popular art, as the term indicates, is an art of the people, *by* the people—but not necessarily *for* the people.

Why is this so? For one thing, the popular artist's neighbors, lacking his instinct for expressing his visions directly, are apt to want his images to conform to conventional photographic norms. Collectors of popular art, on the other hand, are sophisticated enough to know that art never settles for mere imitations of life, and are therefore delighted by the imaginative shortcuts the popular artist takes without being aware that he is taking them. Picasso loved Rousseau not for what the "Douanier" thought he was doing, but for what he actually did.

In recent decades popular art has indeed become "popular." It now appeals to that very large audience of the affluent that is indifferent to or offended by the cerebral "put-ons" of the avant-garde. Sensing quite clearly that modern art has lost touch with modern life, that it is produced by an "in" group contemptuous of communicating common joys and griefs, and that its values are inflated artificially by an establishment with an enormous vested interest in the status quo, this new public is searching eagerly for an escape from the prevailing sterility.

More than twenty-five years ago André Malraux, then the most admired spokesman of the avant-garde, put his finger on the dilemma. "As modern art forges ahead," he wrote, "it seems to become more and more indifferent to what art signified, whether deliberately or not, during untold ages: a form of man's awareness of the world. The sculptors of the Acropolis and the cathedrals, the painter of the Villeneuve Pietà, Michelangelo, Titian and Rembrandt really 'possessed' a world; is not our art, born of a cleavage of man's consciousness, tending to possess no more than its private kingdom? . . ."

Twenty-five years later, in the last year of his life and still looking for a way out of this intellectual cul-de-sac, Malraux came to Haiti and found what he had been looking for.

The First Generation (1945–1957)

Malraux was not the first European intellectual to fall in love with Haitian popular art. André Breton, the surrealist ideologue, had visited Port-au-Prince in 1946, bought several small pictures by the *vaudou* priest Hector Hyppolite (fig. 120), and exposed them in the first

120. *Hector Hyppolite (1947).*

UNESCO show with the prediction that they would revolutionize modern art. "It needs revolutionizing," Breton added (plate 33).

That was the year that Haitian popular art appeared out of nowhere. Two years earlier, in 1944, an American watercolorist on a wartime assignment to teach English to the Haitians had opened Le Centre d'Art in Port-au-Prince. His name was DeWitt Peters. Astonished to find no contemporary painting or sculpture in the country with the Caribbean's richest culture and most romantic history, Peters announced classes in painting, drawing, modeling, and ceramics. He got the surprise of his life. On the doors of a bar in Montrouis, prophetically called *Ici la renaissance* (Here is the renaissance), the first paintings by Hector Hyppolite were sighted (fig. 121). Artists with styles of their own began bringing their offerings to Peters. Until then, what little they had painted had elicited nothing but derision from the mulatto élite, accustomed to buying in Paris what art their homes contained. A marketplace had miraculously appeared. Peters not only liked what he saw, he bought it, and began to sell it to jaded American art lovers.

Before the opening of Le Centre d'Art, the only works that could be described as popular art were two or three watercolors on paper by

121. Bar "Ici la Renaissance," Montrouis (1947).

an artist who remembered what King Henry Christophe's palace had looked like in the early 1800s (fig. 123). There were, however, other visible signs of artistic activity—signs that only waited to be seen by eyes prepared to see them. Just as travelers crisscrossing Africa for centuries had never so much as hinted at the existence of one of the world's great sculptural styles, so visitors to Haiti (even Haitians themselves) professed never to have seen the vivid pictographs painted on the thatched-roof adobe huts the peasants call *cailles*, from Jeremie in the southwest to Ouanaminthe in the northeast. Only after the "renaissance" had erupted were they noticed and photographed (fig. 122).

122. Pictographs on peasant *caille near Jeremie* (1948).

123. Numa Desroches, Sans Souci Palace, Milot, Haiti, c. 1808–20. André Wauters Gallery, New York.

Why was it that these wall decorations, unlike the paintings to come, were predominantly abstract? Probably because they were related to the sign language of *vaudou*, the *vever* (fig. 124). Precise geometrical symbols of the particular *loas* (spirits) to be invoked, the *vevers* (symbolic diagrams) are drawn on the earthen floor with flour or ashes from the hand of the *houngan* (priest of the cult) before a ceremony can properly begin. A strange business, these *vevers*. Unlike the other manifestations of the cult—hypnotic drumming, consecration of fetishes, blood sacrifice of animals, "possession"—the *vever* seems to have had no origin in the African homeland. Where then did it come from? From the curlicues, compass points, and "eyes" the Masons use in their rituals? Perhaps. Or from Indian sand painting?

The method of making the designs is very similar to that practiced by American Indians in the southwestern United States (see p. 53). We don't *know* that the gentle Arawaks, who inhabited Hispaniola before Columbus and his Spanish bullies exterminated them, made sand paintings. Even if they did, it may be romantic to suppose that the Africans imported to replace them in the sixteenth century preserved the tradition and guarded it secretly throughout the next two centuries when all Indians had vanished from Haiti—yet they may have.

124. Vevers, *Croix-des-Missions (1954)*.

Vaudou, the tribal religion, was enriched by the century and a half of isolated independence that followed the expulsion of the French in 1804. It was enriched, too, by its coexistence with Christianity. Identifying Damballa, the Dahomean serpent god, with St. Patrick; the warlike Ogouns, slayers of dragons, with St. Jacques and St. George; Erzili, goddess of love, with the Virgin Mary, and so forth, the *houngan* was not merely adapting his spirits to the white man's prestigious saints; he was recognizing, in many cases, qualities of gentleness and mercy that complemented the more earthy, erotic powers of his own deities.

Fertile as Haiti's culture was, however, there is no reason to believe that painting and sculpture would have flowered spontaneously. A catalyst was needed—someone who believed in the possibility enough to make it happen. And a market—an institution that would convince talented Haitians that art was not only a respectable occupation but could be a better way of making a living than sweeping a yard, driving a taxi, or even sacrificing a goat to Agoué, god of the sea. Peters was that catalyst and the Centre d'Art was that marketplace. Within a year or two, five painters of genius had emerged.

Hector Hyppolite was the first to achieve fame and the first to die—his painting career spanned little more than three years. A *houngan* from St. Marc, he painted visionary portraits of the *loas* (fig. 125) with an utter disregard for perspective and conventional composition

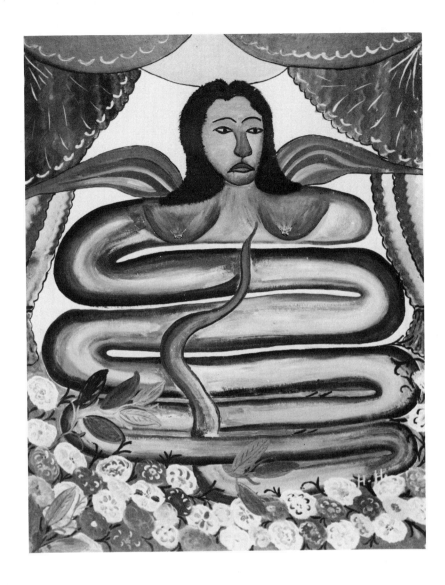

125. *Hector Hyppolite, Snake Goddess (Aida Wedo). Private collection.*

and color. So vivid were Hyppolite's dreams, however, and so commanding his personality that he carried everything before him (figs. 126, 127). Once, in fact, a large crowd bore his latest picture in triumph through the streets. The last time this had happened, someone remarked, was during the early decades of the Italian Renaissance.

Shortly before Hyppolite's death in the summer of 1948 I watched him working on two paintings of women, subtly put together with none of the harshness of color so shocking in his early work. As in most of the *houngan's* pictures, the sky had been deftly bypassed. The floral background of the first picture—a nude coiled sensuously on a sofa, being admired by two maids in bathing suits—was spotlighted by vignettes probably suggested by the designs on toilet-water labels. Hyppolite commented on the second picture, lovers on a couch: "She looks as if she refuses, but she consents." This eroticism manifest in so many of the artist's pictures was reflected in the way he would spend a typical day. He would rise at six, put his troupe to work building a fishing boat or preparing food, and then wander over to the Centre d'Art "to pay my respects to Mr. Peters." Returning to paint without

126. Hector Hyppolite, Mounted Ogoun. Collection Jason Seley, Cornell, N.Y.

127. Hector Hyppolite, Ceremony. Collection Bishop Alfred Voegeli, New York.

interruption from nine to twelve, he would then take in a movie at the Rex Theatre with Rigaud Benoit, his inseparable companion. "I like all kinds of movies," he said, "American, French, Spanish, so long as they're about love. Love pictures inspire me. Love is very important to an artist. You know the way one caresses a beautiful girl? That's the way I caress a tableau."

Truman Capote, whom I took to see him at that time, was struck by the naturalness of Hyppolite's environment and by the way his personality dissolved one's sense of isolation from man and nature. He found Hyppolite's art admirable, he said, "because there's nothing in it that has been slyly transposed; he is using what lives inside him, his country's spiritual history, sayings and worship." It reminded the young novelist of an old man he had encountered on a bus the day before who wore a carnival mask and claimed to have made the sky. "I suppose you made the moon too?" another passenger observed scornfully, to which the old man had replied, "And the stars, they are my grandchildren." A rowdy woman clapped her hands and announced that the man was crazy. "My dear lady," he responded, "if I am crazy how could I have made these beautiful things?"

Philomé Obin of Cap Haïtien (fig. 128) was Hyppolite's exact opposite in temperament. His paintings, put together as though designed by Euclid, depicted Haiti's turbulent history in colors of pearl gray,

128. Philomé Obin (1962).

129.

129. *Philomé Obin,* Funeral of Charlemagne Péralte, *1922 (1946). Collection the author.*

130. *Street in Cap Haïtien where Obin glimpsed funeral for Péralte.*

130.

robin's-egg blue, and rose (figs. 129, 130). Protestant, orderly, meticulous as a carpenter ant, this solid citizen of the North believed he was demonstrating in his art "correct" precepts, imbibed from a French drawing master who had passed briefly through the former capital of the French colony when the artist was very young. Hyppolite's ex-

131.

132.

131. *Philomé Obin,* Revolutionary Cabinet of 1915 Awaiting Arrival of Wounded. *Musée d'Art Haïtien.*

132. *Philomé Obin,* F. D. Roosevelt Interceding in the Beyond for the Peace of the Americas. *Private collection.*

pressionism had resembled in many ways what the modern artist does to escape the past at any cost, and his admirers had been delighted to discover Van Gogh's tormented trees or de Kooning's fractured women in the paintings by the visionary *houngan*—so that many of them made the mistake of dismissing Obin's equally sovereign work as the uninspired prose of a provincial putterer. Failing to understand the sterility of the academic tradition—or exactly how he has sidestepped its traps—Obin has always insisted that he is painting by the book. Once when he was working on his *Crucifixion* in the apse of the Cathedral St. Trinité (see frontispiece), I asked him why a figure in the foreground was half the size of one farther back and he replied quite seriously: "To demonstrate the classical laws of perspective."

No other Haitian popular artist had ever heard of the classical laws of perspective, and Philomé Obin is proud of his superior education. Either because he forgot what he had been taught during the fallow decades that preceded the opening of the Centre d'Art, or because his art made its own laws, Obin painted like Obin from the moment his first picture was sold. He has never deviated from that magic realism which all Cap Haïtien painters now emulate in their various ways (fig. 133). When he paints a religious picture it calls to mind Simone Martini or Fra Angelico because its piety is rendered with the same fidelity to barnyard or manger (fig. 134A). His best portraits recall Antonello da Messina or Botticelli because his subjects are treated with the same di-

133. Dieudonné Pluviose, Christophe Burning Cap Haïtien. *Collection the author.*

INCENDIE DU CAP   D. PLUVIOSE

134A.

134B.

134C.

134A. *Philomé Obin,* Nativity *(1960). Collection Mrs. Nathan Alexander.*

134B. *Philomé Obin,* Portrait of Mme Antenor Firmin. *Collection the author.*

134C. *Senêque Obin,* Tenue à l'Extraordinaire (Masonic Assembly)*. Collection Oscar de Mejo.*

rectness, sobriety and psychological penetration (fig. 134B). The paintings of Philomé's brother, the late Senêque Obin, are as original and sometimes more startling (fig. 134C).

Castera Bazile began to paint when he was Peters's houseboy.

From the very beginning his sensitivity and devout inclinations led him to subjects that had no appeal to Hyppolite or Obin: a woman being delivered of a child (fig. 135), a peasant woman fatalistically contemplating her undernourished children (plate 35), a peasant-style *Adoration* (fig. 136). When Bazile painted *vaudou* or Catholic subjects—as with most Haitian peasants the two pervasive cults merged in his mind—he brought out their human aspects without sacrificing their sense of mystery (fig. 137).

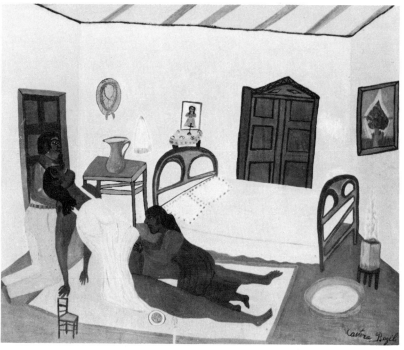

135. Castera Bazile, The Delivery. *Collection Marlene Barash.*

136. Castera Bazile with Adoration of Virgin *(1948).*

137. Castera Bazile, Triumph *(1949). Collection Edward Bragaline.*

135.

136.

137.

Rigaud Benoit's art has never faltered from 1946 (fig. 138) to the present. Essentially an anecdotalist, he illuminates whatever is bizarre and pretentious in Haitian life, but with a comic sense that by some miracle of pictorial tact stops short of caricature or sententiousness. The viewer—whether he is contemplating *vaudou*, a cockfight, a shipwreck, a bourgeois masquerade ball (plate 37), or a wedding interrupted by a jealous woman tearing the clothes off the bride at the altar (fig. 139)—is always conscious first that he is looking at a work of art.

Every time I have complimented Benoit on a new masterpiece, his

139. Rigaud Benoit, The Interrupted Marriage. Collection the author.

answer has invariably been, *"C'est magnifique, n'est ce pas? Magnifique!"* And why not? Should he express modesties or doubts he doesn't feel? He is not reticent about providing scenarios for what he paints, either; not for him the modern artist's wish to make you feel that his hand is guided by some force over which he has no control. *The Shipwreck,* he told me, depicts the moment when the survivors must choose between the offerings of La Sirène, *vaudou* sea spirit, and the mortal ship speeding to their rescue. "Those who wait for the ship will wait in vain. The ship will break up and they'll be eaten by the sharks" (figs. 140, 141).

In his paintings of the last decade Benoit has moved without

140. *Rigaud Benoit,* The Shipwreck. *Collection Issa el Saieh.*

141. *Rigaud Benoit, drawing for a later version of* The Shipwreck. *Collection the author.*

142. Rigaud Benoit with painting of ceremony at tree (1973).

143.

breaking stride from the anecdotal to the mystical. A painting of 1973 (figs. 142, 143) in which the possessed appear as shadows in the shallows gives way to the *Calice* of 1980, an almost abstract parable of life out of death (fig. 144).

Last of the quintet of masters of the first generation was Wilson Bigaud (fig. 145), a Haitian Brueghel who in the late fifties suffered a

143. Detail of painting in figure 142.

144. Rigaud Benoit, Calice (1980). Neiswanger Collection, Davenport (Iowa) Art Gallery.

145. Wilson Bigaud with painting (1949).

144.

145.

119

nervous breakdown from which his art has never recovered. It was brought on in part by an accumulation of sudden wealth he didn't know how to spend, and in part by confusing unsolicited advice about how to join the "mainstream" of international surrealism and abstraction. In 1957 Bigaud made one last, valorous attempt to "get with it" (fig. 146). A guitar, its strings cut and forming a spiderweb, is spewing out a fish; a living flower grows through the artist's foot and the serpents of Damballa sprout from the unlikeliest places. Evidently realizing it was no use, Bigaud stopped painting for almost a decade. At the height of his powers (1951–55) cock thieves, whores, roisterers in Mardi Gras and Ra-Ra, musicians, politicians, *serviteurs* of the African *mystères* all pass in review, held together by Bigaud's fascination with action and his ability to "freeze" it within a frame (plate 36, fig. 147).

146. Wilson Bigaud, Conflicts and Tensions *(1957). San Francisco Museum of Art.*

147. Wilson Bigaud, Sacrifice of the Cock *(1954). Collection the author.*

149.

148.

The subtleties of Bigaud's departures from "objective truth" may be seen in the *Self-Portrait in Mardi Gras Costume*, which he painted from a photograph I'd taken of him in the doorway of his *caille* in Bolosse in 1954. The antlers, peacock plumes, sequined blouse, earrings, nosering, stippled face, and fantasized "artist's palette" are all fused into a great image by the down-to-earth "reality" of the tennis shoes and the hypnotic fear reflected in the wide-open eyes (figs. 148, 149).

148. Wilson Bigaud, Self-Portrait in Mardi Gras Costume. Collection Milwaukee Art Center.

149. Wilson Bigaud in Mardi Gras costume in doorway of his caille, Bolosse (1954).

Murals: From the Centre d'Art Jeep to the Cathedral Ste. Trinité

Late in 1948, as Codirector of Le Centre d'Art, I proposed to DeWitt Peters a way of countering the flight of Haiti's artistic capital abroad. All the important pictures by the five artists described above were being bought by collectors in the United States. Soon there would be nothing left in Haiti to prove that this "renaissance," as it was being called, had ever happened. The Centre d'Art jeep, decorated from hood to tailgate with "murals" by Bigaud, Benoit, Bazile, and the others, gave me an idea. (The jeep invariably evoked derision in the

150. Centre d'Art jeep, DeWitt Peters at the wheel (1948).

151. Murals in apse of Cathedral Ste. Trinité (1949). Detail of lower section with tempera paintings by Benoit, Philomé Obin, and Brazile.

streets from the same people who, twenty years later, would have regarded the owner of any *camion* or "tap-tap" not so decorated as hopelessly out of step.) "They must paint murals," I said to Peters. "Walls can't be moved." Peters agreed. The government was planning a Bicentennial Exposition but the funds for murals had already been allocated to *pompiers* from Belgium and France. The Breton Archbishop of the Roman Catholic Church, whom I approached next, shook his head. Let loose these peasants, most of whom worshiped the "demons of *vaudou*," in his spotless cathedral? Impossible! But there was another church, the smaller Protestant Episcopal Cathedral Ste. Trinité, a couple of blocks away and similarly bare. Its bishop, C. Alfred Voegeli, was enthusiastic: "We'll provide the scaffolds and artists' fees, you provide the artists and direction."

Work began in December of 1949 and the apse murals were completed six weeks later (fig. 151 and frontispiece). But during the whole preceding year a score of artists had painted experimental murals in the Centre d'Art to determine who could handle the chosen medium (egg tempera) and translate best to large surfaces the images hitherto realized on small pieces of Masonite. William Calfee, a Washington, D.C., painter-sculptor whom I had come to know during the War, became technical advisor to this phase of the project.

A large upstairs room was turned over to the "sophisticated" artist—for Peters had not yet abandoned the idea that art education could produce artists. The basement walls and ceilings, supported by massive square pillars, were turned over to the self-taught. Obin, older than the others and disdaining to compete with them, painted in solitary grandeur a mural overlapping adjoining walls in the upstairs library (fig. 152). The other artists upstairs went through paroxysms of indecision and despair. One would mount a stepladder, apply a daub of paint, contemplate it from the floor, and then remount to erase. Another projected a drawing on his wall with a magic lantern and attempted to fill it in. A third had a nervous breakdown. A fourth, in his frustration, gave up painting entirely. Downstairs, in contrast, there was no indecision at all. The walls were attacked with abandon. The images were convincing. One day a derisive scrawl in a primitive hand appeared on the privy wall: *Les artistes de l'étage ne sont pas même des préliminaires primitives.*

Benoit, Obin, and Bazile were finally selected to paint the three panels of the forty-foot-high apse. Gabriel Levêque, who had painted Giotto-like angels in the basement, rounded out the tripartite design with cherubim dropping flowers from triumphal wreaths. Benoit's *Nativity* was predictably anecdotal. I asked him one day why a *marchande* peddling pineapples to the Holy Family had only one arm. "Yaws" was his laconic answer. Obin and Bazile solved practical problems as characteristically. Obin in his central *Crucifixion* depicted the crowd behind the Cross as typical city folk on a Sunday outing enjoying a spectacle, no more involved in this tragedy than an American crowd in the thirties observing a lynching in the Deep South, or a German one in the same decade taking in the torching of a synagogue. Bazile, faced with the more difficult problem of bringing a supernatural

event, the *Ascension*, down to earth, humanized it by showing two boys kicking a soccer ball in the street below.

Bishop Voegeli, who had been away from Haiti during the painting of the apse, exclaimed to me when he entered the cathedral: "Thank God they painted Haitians!" It had been the only directive I'd given the artists. Once accepted, there would be no chance that they might fall back on traditional chromos. The Haitian public was a little shocked by what it saw, but not enough to argue with the worldwide publicity that greeted the opening. One of the first to see the completed apse, the American philanthropist Mrs. Vincent Astor, donated funds for the completion of the work.

Among the seven artists who participated in the second round of murals (1950–51), the star was Wilson Bigaud. His mural, covering the cathedral's largest wall, depicted *The Marriage at Cana*, with Christ turning the water into wine (fig. 153). Moonlight floods a graveyard in the top distance past which a procession straggles downhill to the marriage party in the foreground. Backlighted in the acid-green gloaming, cock thieves are being pursued by the rural police through the branches of a giant tree. Around a similar forest giant on the right move Ra-Ra (Lenten) celebrants beating drums, blowing bamboo *vaccines,* reed flutes and conch shells. The very-bourgeois bride and groom seem not at all impressed by the miracle being performed in front of them by the Son of God. The village tart with her shopping purse, the young blade smoking a cigarette in his rocker, and the naked boy contemplating the stuck pig on a banana leaf are too absorbed in their mundane thoughts to take any notice.

I had asked Préfèt DuFaut, whose bizarre pictographs on his *caille* near Jacmel had brought him to my attention the year before, to paint two murals in the south transept. One of them reflected the many *Streets of Jacmel* that were already one of this peasant artist's favorite subjects (plate 43) and the other followed the pattern of pictures de-

152. Philomé Obin, trial mural in library of old Centre d'Art (1948).

153. Wilson Bigaud, Detail from Marriage at Cana, *Cathedral Ste. Trinité (1950). Charcoal.*

154. *Préfèt DuFaut, Trésors de Reine Titane (c. 1950). Collection Mr. and Mrs. Lloyd Siegel.*

155. *André Pierre, Images of Vaudou. Collection Issa el Saieh.*

picting *loas* on balls or pinnacles surrounded by ceremonial banners (fig. 154). As in the case of all the other artists, the idea was to achieve a synthesis of the images each gravitated toward naturally.

The Second Generation (1957–1972)

A second generation of artists matured during the late fifties and achieved fame in the sixties. This was the period during which President François ("Papa Doc") Duvalier became so embroiled politically with President John F. Kennedy that Haiti was virtually sealed off from tourism. One result of this enforced isolation was that the older artists were turned in upon their own resources. Another consequence was that new artists developed their styles with no thought of sales to influence their direction. Like the stars of the first generation, it was to their advantage to have been born, so to speak, underground.

Most original and first to achieve fame abroad was André Pierre, who could be called Hyppolite's heir (fig. 156). Like Hyppolite, Pierre was a priest of *vaudou* who began to paint in middle age and had a unique style. To an even greater extent than Hyppolite—who did occasionally paint a still life or a portrait—Pierre painted the symbolic appearances of the African spirits exclusively. Less expressionistically, but with more control and consistency, Pierre revealed his gorgeously arrayed *loas* and their worshipers in jungle settings of sinuous density (plate 40). One may speculate that his trees with amputated limbs derived from Bigaud's mural in Ste. Trinité but certainly the human and superhuman cast was wholly of the artist's imagining, and the tapestry-like assembly of images unprecedented (fig. 155).

Pierre's first paintings were done inside the hollowed calabash

halves used in *houmfors* to contain offerings to the *loas* or the blood of sacrificed animals. The particular *houmfor* where Pierre officiated in the fifties (and next to which he still lives and paints) is at Croix-des-Missions. When not officiating, Pierre decorated *vaudou* vessels or designed ceremonial flags (fig. 157). The late Maya Deren, American dancer-cinematographer whose book *Divine Horsemen* was to become the first intimate study of the cult, showed the shells to Nancy Heinl, wife of the commander of the American military training mission to the Haitian government. The two women encouraged Pierre to paint his flamboyant *loas* on flat surfaces, and in the first of these paintings the oval frame of the half calabash is still retained (fig. 158).

At about the same time (or earlier, according to the artist, whose sense of time is not necessarily reliable), Pierre painted murals for the inner sanctuary of the Croix-des-Missions *houmfor*. There is a transcendental magic about these wall paintings, with their legendary symbolism of birds, fish, calyces, urns, and crosses, that has reminded more than one visitor of the early Christian murals in the Roman catacombs (fig. 159). Be that as it may, Pierre was soon receiving so many commissions for paintings that his ritual obligations lapsed entirely.

156. *André Pierre at Croix-des-Missions in the 1960s.*

159. *André Pierre, mural at Croix-des-Missions, detail (late 1950s).*

158. *André Pierre, early painting of Guédé retaining calabash shape. Ex-collection Chris Borgen.*

157. *André Pierre, ceremonial sequined flags, Croix-des-Missions.*

161. *Georges Liautaud at his forge, Croix-des-Bouquets (late 1960s).*

160. *André Pierre,* Maîtresse La Siréne. *Collection Milwaukee Art Center.*

Perhaps for this reason, when the high priest at the *houmfor* died in 1978, Pierre, though next in line to succeed him, was passed over. At once Pierre began building his own shrine within a few feet of the offensive old one, but the new *houngan* retaliated by declining to show visitors André's murals!

If a cult as casual as *vaudou* can be said to have a center, the village of Croix-des-Bouquets a few miles to the east, where Pierre had also painted murals in the late fifties, is that center. And here another artist of similar age and as great originality surfaced at about the same time—a blacksmith, whose name was Georges Liautaud (fig. 161). His iron crosses, with embellishments deriving from *vaudou's* cabalistic flour drawings, had been observed in local graveyards (fig. 162). Liautaud was sought out and persuaded to forge nonutilitarian sculptures. Some of these were free-standing (fig. 163), others were designed to hang on walls, and still others were metal "windows" punctured with intricate patterns to diffuse the sunlight (fig. 164). These works, perhaps the most innovative in sculpture since Calder's mobiles, now grace such prestigious institutions as the Museums of Modern Art in Paris and New York and the Musée d'Art Haïtien in Port-au-Prince (fig. 165).

Other talented metal sculptors, notably the Louisjuste brothers of Croix-des-Bouquets, Murat Brierre (fig. 166), and Damien Paul, followed in Liautaud's wake. And soon the Caribbean, followed by the rest of the world, was inundated with an art form as ubiquitous as the grotesque carnival mask.

162.

166.

163.

162. Georges Liautaud, cross. Collection the author.

163. Georges Liautaud, Aida Wedo. Collection Pierre Monosiet, Bizoton, Haiti.

164. Georges Liautaud, The Tree of Life. Collection the author.

165. Georges Liautaud, Hermaphroditic Demon. Musée d'Art Haïtien, Port-au-Prince.

166. Murat Brierre, Demon-loa Riding a Cow. Private collection.

165.

164.

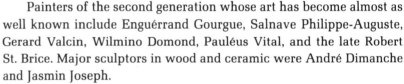

167. *Enguerrand Gourgue, The Magic Table. Oil on cardboard. Inter-American Fund, Museum of Modern Art, New York.*

Painters of the second generation whose art has become almost as well known include Enguérrand Gourgue, Salnave Philippe-Auguste, Gerard Valcin, Wilmino Domond, Pauléus Vital, and the late Robert St. Brice. Major sculptors in wood and ceramic were André Dimanche and Jasmin Joseph.

Gourgue, who while still a boy in the late forties painted for me an unprecedented picture (*The Magic Table*, fig. 167), is a special case. Elements of surrealism had already crept into his precocious style and these he developed with technical bravura to explore *vaudou*'s darker aspects—resuscitation of the dead (*zombis*), nightmares induced by sorcerers (*bocors*), visitations from werewolves (*loup-garous*). From Spain, where he now lives, Gourgue continues to influence some of the younger artists with his "diabolic" and fluid imagery.

Philippe-Auguste, a retired judge of the élite class in the capital who took up painting in the early sixties, adapted Henri Rousseau's jungle precisionism to the Haitian scene, sometimes including in his subtly patterned pictures such nonindigenous fauna as zebras, giraffes, and hippopotami. His early pictures (plate 34, fig. 168) glowed with a radiance as irresistible as his French model's, but later attempts to project such surreal images as hermaphrodites with three sets of arms were not always so convincing.

Gerard Valcin, a tile setter from Port-au-Prince, Wilmino Domond, a young coffee planter from Marbial, and Pauléus Vital, a fisherman from Jacmel, were realists whose reportage of the local scene usually escaped banality by the intensity of their observation and color. In such a painting as Domond's early (1965) *David Slaying the Lion*, the innocent conviction with which the rural Haitian scene is rendered makes the biblical story live anew (fig. 169). Vital's *Ceremony for Ogoun* (plate 42) is just as firmly based upon the landscape around Jacmel but is given a metaphorical spirit transcending place and time.

168. *Salnave Philippe-Auguste,* Two Mermaids. *Collection the author.*

III
Afro-America: Haiti and Brazil

33. Hector Hyppolite, The Three-Eyed King.
Musée d'Art Haïtien, Port-au-Prince.

34. Salnave Philippe-Auguste, Two Mermaids.
Collection the author.

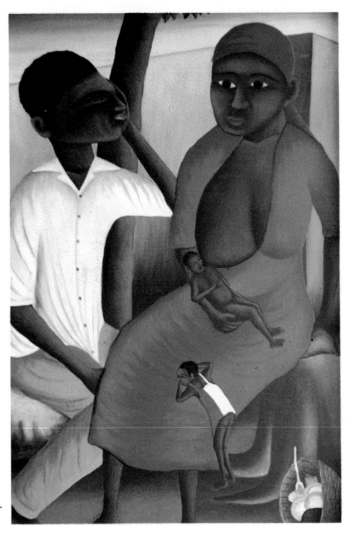

35. *Castera Bazile, Peasant Family. Private collection.*

36. *Wilson Bigaud, Papa Zaca. Private collection.*

37. Rigaud Benoit, Bal du Carnival. Neiswanger Collection, Davenport (Iowa) Art Gallery.

38. Rigaud Benoit, Seated Woman. Private collection.

39. Michel Sinvil, Crucifixion. Painted papier-mâché. Renaissance II, Jacmel.

40. André Pierre, Ceremony for the Forest-God. Collection the author.

41. *Roland Blain. Eve and the Crocodiles. Collection Marvin Liebman.*

42. *Pauléus Vital, Ceremony for Ogoun. Private collection.*

43. *Préfèt DuFaut, Harbor and Streets of Jacmel. Private collection.*

44. *St. Louis Blaise, The Time of the Gourds. Collection the author.*

45. Prosper Pierre-Louis, Loas. Collection the author.

46. Lafortune Félix, Mambo with Telephone Poles. Collection the author.

47. *Djanira da Mota e Silva, Angel in Tennis Shoes. Estate of the artist, Samambaia, Brazil.*

48. *Julio Martins da Silva, Crystal Palace, Rio de Janeiro. Private collection.*

49. *Gerson de Souza, The King and Eye. Collection the author.*

47.

49.

48.

50. José Antonio da Silva, Stations of the Cross. Nossa Senhora do Sogrado Coracão, São José do Rio Préto, Brazil.

51. Fernando V. da Silva, Bordello No. 2. Collection the author.

IV
Indians Once Under Spain

52. Masked figure in devil dance. Puno, Bolivia. University Gallery, University of Florida.

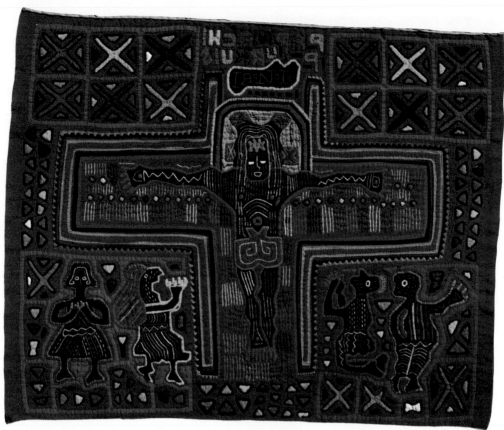

53. *Crucifixion mola. Collection Ann Parker and Avon Neal, North Brookfield, Mass.*

54. *Space vehicle mola. From Parker and Neal, Molas.*

55. Zut. Man's head cloth from Nahualá, Guatemala. Collection the author.

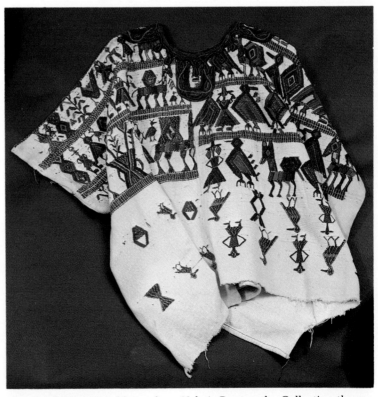

56. Huipil. Woman's blouse from Nebaj, Guatemala. Collection the author.

57. Santo. Polychrome wood and metal, Guatemala. Collection the author.

58. Mario Tulio Villalobos, Benediction. Cali, Colombia. Collection Daniel Storper, New York.

59. Primitivo Evan Poma, Sarhua, Peru. Hinchaway. Collection the author.

60. Alberid Zdaquira, Fiesta. Cotopaxi, Ecuador. Collection the author.

61. *Chael, Fishing Village, Lake Nicaragua. Collection the author.*

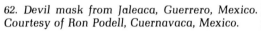

62. *Devil mask from Jaleaca, Guerrero, Mexico. Courtesy of Ron Podell, Cuernavaca, Mexico.*

63. *José Benítez Sánchez, The Dismemberment of Tacutsi Nakawé. Yarn painting. Courtesy Juan Negrin, Guadalajara, Mexico.*

64. *Marcial Camilo Ayala, Nocturnal Fiesta. Collection the author.*

65. Juan Camilo Ayala, Fiesta with Volcanoes and Angels. Private collection.

66. *Marcial Camilo Ayala, Self-Portrait. Collection Galeria Lara, Cuernavaca, Mexico.*

67. Felix Jiménez Chino, *Lovers. Collection the author.*

68. Marcial Camilo Ayala, The Wave. MIND Collection, Norwalk, Conn.

69. Marcial Camilo Ayala, What the Sun Sees. Collection the author.

169. Wilmino Domond, David Slaying the Lion (1965). Collection the author.

St. Brice, like Gourgue, was another very special case. He began to paint his *vaudou*-induced dreams with the encouragement of a young abstract artist from New York, Alex John, who boarded with him at Bizoton in the early fifties. His free-floating apparitions (fig. 170), rendered with dots of color, had a posthumous progeny in the work of the "Saint Soleil" peasant commune (fig. 171) which Malraux admired during his visit to Haiti in the summer of 1977. The mystique of this commune, set forth by the two intellectuals of the élite who organized it, is that any peasant art offered for sale becomes tainted by commer-

170. Robert St. Brice, Three Queens (c. 1960). Oil. Collection the author.

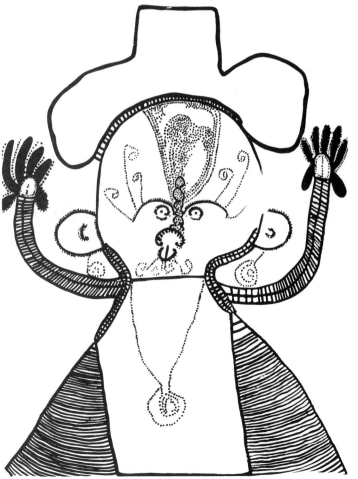

171. Saint-Soleil (anon.), Apparition (c. 1975). Silkscreen print after drawing in ink. Private collection.

172. *Louisiane Saint-Fleurant, Mambo with Flowers. Petit Gallery, Pétion-Ville, Haiti.*

173. *Prosper Pierre-Louis, Loas. Marassa Gallery, Petion-Ville, Haiti.*

cialism. But ironically the two artists Malraux admired most, Prosper Pierre-Louis and Louisiane Saint-Fleurant, broke away even before the French critic's book was published posthumously, and have produced their most striking pictures for galleries in Pétionville that pay their artists generously (figs. 172, 173, plate 45).

The Third Generation (1973–   )

It was inevitable that commercialism would begin to nibble away at a popular art so attractive to the buying public of Europe and the Americas. The first telltale sign was the proliferation of pseudo-African wood carvings in the gift shops of Port-au-Prince. Who was to tell unwary buyers that these ugly objects were kitsch, having nothing to do either with African tribal art, which they mimicked, or with genuine Haitian sculpture, which they displaced the way a muddy flood momentarily obliterates a pure rivulet? Tawdry imitations of the old masters of Haitian popular painting were quick to follow, and soon the big Arabian galleries in the capital were crowded from floor to ceiling with gaudy examples of this debased product, authentic works of art occasionally lurking among them.

The surprising fact is that there were as many genuine, innovative talents among the artists of the third generation as there were in the first and second. No fewer than four outstanding sculptors emerged in the late seventies, only one of them part of an ongoing tradition. This one, Serge Jolimeau of Croix-des-Bouquets, towered while still a teenager above the flourishing school of younger metal craftsmen in that *vaudou*-haunted village. Attracting the attention of the Centre d'Art, Jolimeau was encouraged to cut and burnish monumental flat sculptures; some were in layers connected by hooks and chains, one layer seen through another, with mobile appendages (fig. 174). The flowing grace of Jolimeau's profiles—cut, as always in Haitian metal sculpture, from such industrial waste as Esso oil drums—reminds one of Egyptian prototypes (fig. 175), in contrast to the blunt idiom of Liautaud whose spiritual ancestry seems far more archaic (fig. 176). But what was also new in this young sculptor's work was a playful eroticism never before seen in Haitian art: figures part male, part female, incorporating fish and birds that seemed to be feeding on the sexual organs of their hosts.

174. Serge Jolimeau, Androgynous Fantasy. MIND Collection, Norwalk, Conn.

175. Serge Jolimeau, Figure. Collection the author.

176. Georges Liautaud, Woman Carrying Her Crippled Husband (1981). Collection the author.

177. *Georges Laratte, stone head (c. 1975). Collection the author.*

Hardly less freshly conceived were the stone sculptures of Georges Laratte, the papier-mâché figures of Michel Sinvil, and the wood carvings of Nacius Joseph and Versein.

Probably because he was born and raised on the north coast where most of the artifacts of the aboriginal Taino-Arawaks are to be found, Georges Laratte's early work was sometimes taken to be pre-Columbian (fig. 177). The more complex figures and family groups he created in 1978–80 out of native sandstone and river-rounded boulders (figs. 178, 179) gave him the right to be considered Haiti's first original artist in this medium. Michel Monnin, whose gallery in Port-au-Prince specializes in the art of the third generation, shared with Georges Nader and the author in discovering Laratte. His most recent sculptures (fig. 180), carrying the figure into pure abstraction with effortless grace, call to mind Jean Arp's "human concretions" of the 1930s.

178. *Georges Laratte, stone head (c. 1979). Collection James Segreto.*

179. *Georges Laratte, Lovers. Stone. MIND Collection, Norwalk, Conn.*

180. *Georges Laratte, two figurines in white stone. Private collection.*

The unusual talent of Michel Sinvil was brought to light in the late seventies by Pierre Monosiet, director of both the Centre d'Art and the Musée d'Art Haïtien. Until encouraged by Monosiet to try his hand at complex Catholic (plate 39) and *vaudou* subjects, Sinvil was one of hundreds of anonymous craftsmen who had turned out painted papier-mâché masks for Mardi Gras.

Nacius Joseph's wood carvings first appeared in the fall of 1979 and again it was Pierre Monosiet whose keen eye detected latent ge-

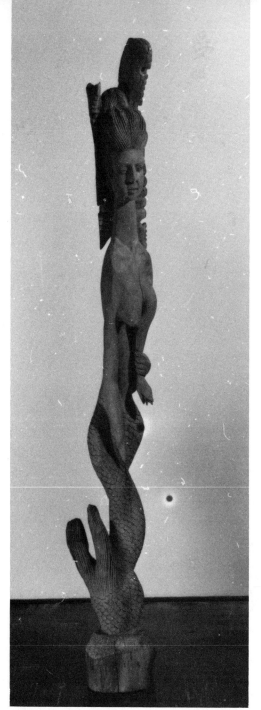

nius. It seems that thirty years before, when Nacius was a boy, he had been an apprentice in the workshop of Odilon Duperier, a wood-carver whose promising career at the Centre d'Art came to an end in the early fifties when he emigrated to the United States. Nacius may also have seen the ceramic beasts and angels of Jasmin Joseph, another talented artist of that period who forsook sculpture for painting at about the time Duperier emigrated, but that is problematical. For a short time he worked with Odilon's brother, Joubert. What Nacius did remember from the Duperiers was their way of leaving part of the block of wood as an "envelope" for the emerging subject, and carving leaves or fruit to enhance the naturalness of the setting.

When Monosiet encountered Nacius Joseph at Petit Goâve in 1979 he had returned to carving again and his first pieces reflected his interests as a shipwright and fisherman in that port. The crude but powerful boatmen in their dugouts would not look out of place beside the Gothic portals of Autun or Vézelay (fig. 181). Then came a more ambitious sculpture, *Murder in the Jungle* (fig. 182), in which two enveloping serpents drink the blood of a decapitated Laocoön-like victim, clearly indicating the artist's familiarity with *vaudou* symbols. A six-foot standing *sirène* of 1980 (fig. 183), in which the sea-goddess draws a serpent's head from her left breast, also has its source in *vaudou* mythology.

183. Nacius Joseph, Metamorphosis of the Sea Loa. *Collection the author.*

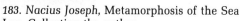

181. Nacius Joseph, Boatmen. *Tropical oak. Renaissance II, Jacmel.*

134

182. Nacius Joseph, Murder in the Jungle. *MIND Collection, Norwalk, Conn.*

184.

185.

186.

Less disturbing but sculpturally just as convincing are Nacius's reliefs. In one dating from 1979, the Virgin (Erzili?) stands on a lamb, splintered to indicate its wool, holding a rose and cross and surmounted by a five-pointed Star of Bethlehem (fig. 184). In another, dating from 1981, various symbols are grouped arbitrarily around an upward-tilted female figure with extraordinary compositional authority (fig. 185).

The only other contemporary Haitian wood-carver with a measure of Nacius's instinct for the medium is George Laratte's son, Versein, whose figures are more "classical" because more knowing (fig. 186).

If the painters of the third generation seem less startlingly original than the sculptors that may be because paintings in Haiti have become as ubiquitous as palm trees. With the exceptions of Gérard Paul (fig. 187) and Camy Rocher (fig. 188), none of these artists seemed as capable as Nacius of making fresh pictorial statements out of the traditional symbols. This may have been because Philippe-Auguste with his exotic jungles, Gourgue with his spooky diabolism, and Obin with his re-creations of Revolutionary history had become so widely known through color postcards as to become almost inescapable influences.

Gourgue's imagery was soon carried into flamboyant new directions by such young artists as the late Celestin Faustin, Madsen Mompremier, Smith Blanchard, and Pierre Augustin. Faustin was not afraid to teeter on the brink of vulgarity, and sometimes went off the deep end. But when his high-colored fantasies worked, no one could conjure up more dramatic dreams of sensual pleasure tinctured with subliminal fears. Before he began to mine this rich lode, Faustin had painted

184. *Nacius Joseph,* Virgin Standing on a Lamb. *Private collection.*

185. *Nacius Joseph,* Relief with Symbols. *Collection the author.*

186. *Versein,* Mourning Figures. *Red Cedar. Collection Mr. and Mrs. William Feldman.*

187. *Gérard Paul, Jonah and the Whale. MIND Collection, Norwalk, Conn.*

188. *Camy Rocher, ceremonial figures with bottles and necklaces. Renaissance II, Jacmel.*

historical and *vaudou* pictures, realistic almost to the point of academicism (fig. 189). But as Gourgue's influence began to affect him, he found his own style. Take *Seduction for Treasure*—depending on one's viewpoint, it is a blue heaven or hell, the skies dripping into grottoes, the trees dripping into gold, supplicants paying for their venal sins whatever price the fleshly spirits ordain, then turning into bats as they vanish in pursuit of their ghostly temptresses (fig. 190).

Philippe-Auguste's predators reappear in the more mysteriously shadowed glades of Roland Blain (plate 41). André Pierre's orderly rites reappear less realistically in the spirit-portraits of the late Camy Rocher, the compositions held together by necklaces, sequined bottles, and candles floating in space but anchored by a "reality" more purely pictorial (fig. 191). The less prolific Cameau Rameau's anchoring de-

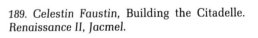

189. Celestin Faustin, Building the Citadelle.
Renaissance II, Jacmel.

190. Celestin Faustin, Seduction for Treasure.
Collection Dr. Ralph Bazin.

191.

192.

191. *Camy Rocher, Mambo. MIND Collection, Norwalk, Conn.*

192. *Cameau Rameau, The Houngan. Galerie Monnin, Port-au-Prince.*

193. *Michel Obin, Battle of Vertières. Private collection.*

vice was dots, evenly spaced as they fall through the canvas like rain or manna from heaven (fig. 192).

In Cap Haïtien no second Obin rose to challenge the ninety-year-old Philomé's undisputed sovereignty, but the vigor of the Obinesque "school" flourishes as never before, not only through Obin's sons, Telemaque, Antoine, and Henri-Claude, but through his great-nephews, Michel (fig. 193) and Jean-Wilner, and such cultivators of the vineyard planted by Philomé and his brother, the late great Senêque, as Pluviose (see fig. 133) and the Bottex brothers, Alcanor, Toussaint,

194. St. Louis Blaise, Ball at the Court of King Henry Christophe. Collection Ralph Bazin.

Fils-Aimé and Edner Jean. More imaginative than these, St. Louis Blaise began by painting monumental evocations of the grandeur of King Henry Christophe's court, sometimes setting them in ballrooms under glittering chandeliers that probably outshine the luxury of even that opulent era (fig. 194). Then, taking a leaf from Gourgue's book, this artist created a series of still lifes, high-keyed in color, subtly shadowed, and with just enough of a touch of Gourgue's ambiguous juxtapositions to give the best of them a disquieting mystery (plate 44, fig. 195A).

Mystery of a different sort surrounded both the emergence and the art of Lafortune Félix in 1980. Like Hyppolite, Félix lives in St. Marc, is a *vaudou* priest in nearby Pont Sondé, started to paint in middle age, and possesses a style of brutal directness. Murals on the exterior wall of his *houmfor* (fig. 195B) led to his discovery. Where did

195A. St. Louis Blaise, The Time of the Gourds. Collection the author.

195B. Lafortune Félix with his Mural of Bossu Trois Cornes, Pont Sondé.

196. *Lafortune Félix, Baron Samedi. Renaissance II, Jacmel.*

197. *Lafortune Félix, Mambo with Telephone Poles. Collection the author.*

Félix come from? Why did he wait so long to paint? What is he telling us? All that can be said at this point is that Félix is a better colorist than the old master and that if he doesn't repeat himself should enjoy as much fame and fortune (figs. 196, 197).

Arts of High Fashion

Luce Turnier and Antonio Joseph were sophisticated painters of great talent, contemporaries of Bigaud and Bazile, who developed their styles abroad without ever losing their emotional identification with the homeland. It was inevitable, when museum acquisitions abroad and high-pressure auctions in New York brought about an escalation of prices among first-generation masters, that arts of high fashion would appear. Haitian collectors, especially, began to vie with one another for the technically brilliant set-pieces of Bernard Séjourné, Emilcar Simil, Jean-René Jérome, and others. Outstanding among them is Raymond Olivier, who has adapted Cubism and Op to visions of the Haitian scene as revealed by diffused sunlight flickering through the lattices of ghostly fin-de-siècle townhouses (fig. 197). One more example of an art which seems, thus far, to be inexhaustible.

Humanity is being progressively sundered from the physical universe.

—CLAUDE LEVI-STRAUSS

The avant-garde is acceptable because it is essentially reactionary.

—JOHN SIMON

When we are no longer children, we are already dead.

—CONSTANTIN BRANCUSI

3
Brazil

EVERY ARTIST SEEMS to impose order on an unruly world. The great artist, by the depth of that penetration, sometimes forecasts change while the philosopher is still asking why and the scientist is explaining how. We have already seen new arts born outside the faltering Western tradition engaged in just such prophetic illuminations. In Brazil—so remote save in its seaboard cities from the West, and so close to those pervasive religious cults which are beginning to bring men back to a harmonious relationship with the natural world—the nature of that new art is being revealed.

It has happened before. By all the historic, cultural, and aesthetic standards of the Graeco-Roman world in the first centuries after Christ, the great art we now call Byzantine was not highly regarded. Historically it flouted the traditional styles of Athens, Pergamum, and Rome. Culturally it bypassed the state religion—that routine worship of the Olympian deities inherited from Greece—celebrating instead the popular underground cults (of which Christianity was one) with their mystical symbolism of otherworldliness. Aesthetically the new popular art was regarded by establishment critics in Rome as childlike, naive, and subversive of good taste. But proponents of this self-taught "primitivism" would have responded that the art of the declining Empire was either formalistic or pornographic, and on all counts the reflection of a decadent society headed for catastrophe.

Parallels with the art world today are so close that only the blindness of those who refuse to admit them is remarkable. Since the specific purpose of this chapter is to examine one of the major seedbeds of the counterculture a side-glance at architecture will illustrate the conflict in values and forms that pervades every society today. The conflict is nowhere more dramatically focused than in Brazil, where the establishment has erected a whole city (Brasília, the new capital) to demonstrate the "purity" of its forms.

Here, in rectangular *supercuadras* of glass so soul-shrinking that even the bureaucrats who are obliged to inhabit them develop paranoid traits, no casual intercourse or creative impulses are possible. Accessible only by private automobile, the city has no walkways for pedestrians; food must be imported; communication is by electronics; and the living quarters of those who provide the labor and services are relegated to rings of satellite communities so distant that visitors are unaware that the majority of the capital's inhabitants live in them.

But even this is not enough to satisfy the establishment, which is in mortal fear of contamination by the lower classes. The popular architecture of the *favelas*, those communities of the poor which have proliferated so naturally in Rio, São Paulo and the other great cities—jerry-built, overlapping, inventive, filled with creative surprises, alive with flowers and the pleasures of community intercourse—is regarded as a threat to the depersonalized technology. So much so that the military government has brought in bulldozers to level the *favelas* and "integrate" their hapless inhabitants in depersonalized apartment blocks miles away from the heart of the city.

How much happier the lot of the popular artists, whose works the establishment attempts to neutralize with patronizing politeness or commercial blandishments but dares not bulldoze into oblivion! The pervasive hostility felt for these artists and their works is often hidden behind such epithets as "innocence," "naiveté," "quaintness," or "childlike charm" with which the engaged art of these modern Byzantines is greeted. This self-protecting stance of an affection tempered by amusement was adopted a hundred years ago when the first popular artist, Henri Rousseau, exhibited his paintings.

As recently as twenty years ago Brazil was still so remote from the trade routes familiar to traveling art critics, so huge in its unexplored regions and teeming cities, that when a European savant, Bihalji-Merin, devoted a massive monograph to the work of *all* the "Masters of Naive Painting" from Rousseau to Obin, he included not a single Brazilian.

Popular art received its grudging quota of recognition in Brazil, nevertheless, at about the same time as elsewhere. Almost coincident with the Museum of Modern Art's pioneering assemblage of popular painters in New York (1938), the first pictures by Heitor Dos Prazeres, Djanira, and José Antonio da Silva were beginning to attract some attention in Brazil. Rousseau's work was already famous enough to give Brazil's first collectors the feeling that it might be prudent to include a "primitive" of local origin.

Dos Prazeres qualified very well indeed. Like the *"Douanier,"* he composed music and poems when he wasn't painting, played an in-

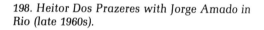

198. Heitor Dos Prazeres with Jorge Amado in Rio (late 1960s).

strument (in his case the guitar), and amused his acquaintances with an earthy sense of humor. Among his friends, as among Rousseau's, were the leading poets and novelists of the day, but no artists. The Brazilian avant-garde contained no painters with the self-assurance of a Gauguin or a Picasso, but the poets and novelists were still close enough to the people to recognize a kindred spirit in the *carioca* samba-composer (fig. 199).

199. Heitor Dos Prazeres, Self-Portrait. Private collection.

What gave Dos Prazeres's pictures their vitality was this artist's deep involvement in the community life of the Rio *favelas* (fig. 200), a life still rich enough to have inspired Vinícius de Moraes to write the scenario on which *Black Orpheus* was based. Participants in Carneval and other street festivals expressed their creativity not only in the words and music of the samba but also in the making of costumes and masks that had yet to be standardized by the requirements of the tourist industry. To what extend Dos Prazeres participated in *macumba*, the Afro-Brazilian cult religion most generally practiced in Rio, is not clear. But as a Brazilian of African ancestry he was surely familiar with its rites. On the whole, though, Dos Prazeres's art, like Pippin's (which it resembles to a startling degree) and Philomé Obin's, was less concerned with interpreting religions and myths than with docu-

200.

201.

200. *Heitor Dos Prazeres, Family in Rio Favela. Private collection.*

201. *Heitor Dos Prazeres, Man on Bicycle Delivering Laundry, Private collection.*

menting the life around him (fig. 201). In this he succeeded. His pictures remain the most vivid record of *carioca* customs and appearances in the first four decades of this century. When Dos Prazeres unexpectedly was given a prize at the 1951 São Paulo Bienal his art was no longer regarded (at least by critics familiar with the art of Rousseau and Pippin) as "crude" or "comical," yet his disdain for perspective and modeling continued to offend the art establishment so that by the time of his death in 1966 this pioneer had been all but forgotten.

We will take a long look at Djanira, José Antonio da Silva, and the other important popular painters who followed in Dos Prazeres's wake; but first the sculptors, whose work relates more directly to African and Indian folk traditions, will afford some insights into what makes Brazil's multiracial culture so fertile a seedbed.

Sculptors of Genius

One major artist appeared during the 428 years between the discovery of Brazil in 1500 and the so-called "Week of Modern Art" in São Paulo that ushered in modernism and art appreciation: Antonio Francisco Lisboa (1738–1814) called Aleijadinho, the Little Cripple. Whether this freed mulatto slave from Minas Gerais was a sophisticated sculptor of unusual sensitivity working within the provincial baroque tradition, or a true popular artist who worked in that tradition because there was no other outlet for his genius, is a matter of opinion—or definition. In any event, Aleijadinho began to work in the style of the craftsmen-carvers who had turned out Catholic ikons for generations without ever creating anything in any way personal. Though his local fame became great in his lifetime, not enough is known about Aleijadinho's personality to determine what motivated his successful search for a

202. Aleijadinho, Prophets at Church of Bom Jesús, Congonhas da Campo. Soapstone.

203A and 203B. Aleijadinho, Stations of the Cross (details) at Congonhas. Polychrome wood.

personal style. Was his nature quickened by the cult religion in which his black mother must have participated during her childhood, and perhaps during his? Did Aleijadinho feel enough resentment toward his white Portuguese masters to make him a rebel, at least to the extent of spurning their routine interpretations of the official religion? Did the agonizing pains he suffered from leprosy in his last years—he had to be rolled to the sculptures with a chisel strapped to the stump of an arm—give him insights into suffering comparable to Beethoven's when that composer was similarly isolated from the world by physical affliction? Whatever the cause, the sculptures of Aleijadinho's final period—the soapstone *Prophets* and polychromed *Stations of the Cross* at Congonhas (fig. 202)—share a monumental serenity with those terminal works of art as memorable for their wisdom as for their artistry.

Only in this century has Aleijadinho's sculpture aroused any serious interest in Brazil, and only in the seventies among connoisseurs abroad. Contemporary scholarship is beginning to recognize that Aleijadinho's innovative departure from baroque norms was deeply rooted in the once-scorned popular wood carvings of Minas (figs. 203A, B). One might suggest, with less plausibility perhaps, that the mulatto sculptor was asserting his racial identity in the only way he could.

I had heard in Salvador, the Bahian capital, that Louco received his sculptor's name because he spent part of every year in a madhouse. I didn't believe it, but I thought Louco might be amused to hear the question. He laughed. "I was a barber until about ten years ago [1966]," he said. "When I stopped shaving heads and started shaving blocks of wood, my neighbors said 'The man is *louco* [crazy].' I couldn't think of a better name for an artist, so I stopped being Boaventura da Silva Filho from that moment."

That was in Cachoeira, a once-prosperous river port on the Paraguaçu some seventy miles west of Salvador where in colonial times the

204. *Louco in his studio, Cachoeira, Brazil (1974).*

205A and 205B. *Candomblé participants, Salvador da Bahia.*

sugarcane cut by slaves was loaded onto barges. Then, as the Empire quietly expired, the slaves were freed. Louco's father was a son of one of those slaves, and here the sculptor was born on January 26, 1932.

From the time when it was the capital of all Brazil until right down to the present, Salvador has been the fountainhead of the transplanted African cultures. Then and now, *candomblé*, the purest, most stylized, and most "African" of the Brazilian cult religions, flourished in this most exotic of Brazilian cities as nowhere else. Louco, whether he was ever a true believer or not, was nourished by the folklore surrounding *candomblé*, attended its gorgeous rites (figs. 205A, B), and saw some of the "miracles," physical and psychic, among those followers of the *Māe de Santo* who believed strongly enough to be "entranced."

Just as *vaudou* is a transplant from Dahomey on the African west coast, so *candomblé*—similar in almost every respect and even sharing some of the same gods—was brought over by slaves from the Yoruba and Nago tribes to the south of Dahomey. Neither religion encouraged image-making, though all the original African tribes shared in the great enterprise of carving fetishes from wood; in fact the only visual art commonly practiced in both transplanted cults is abstract and geometrical. How, then, did the cult religion help to inspire a figurative artist like Louco when none of its imagery was figurative? By what route and through what forms was such a mysterious connection effected? Writing of Haitian art, Pierre Apraxine comes to grips with this paradox: "For the voodoo worshipper nothing is invisible, nothing is in need of representation. There is no supernatural world because all worlds—the immediate and the beyond—are simultaneously present, natural and accessible to the eye." But how was this culture able to move "from the absence of visual art to the concentrated activity of painting convincing enough to attract world attention?" The answer, Apraxine goes on, "may lie in the fact that the absence of visual art among the Haitian masses depended, for the most part, on a state of cohesive and undifferentiated consciousness subsumed under the voodoo religion: individual and collective identity were one and the same." In contrast to the popular masters of other countries who were isolated one from another and were mainly reacting against the fragmented consciousness of technologized societies whose arts were detached from life, the artists of Haiti were making the transition from the invisible state of folkways to the formal visions of individual painters:

They were moving *away* from the undifferentiated consciousness of the collective life toward the individuality of paintings by which they were identified. What a Douanier Rousseau and Obin share as "naive" painters is their totally individual styles, while siphoning their images from the collective consciousness and their inspiration from the real or imagined life of the people.

Substitute Fernando V. da Silva for Obin, or Louco for Liautaud, and the interpretation applies to Brazil as exactly as to Haiti. As with Liautaud (see p. 126), there is no trace of the symbolic abstractions of the transplanted African cults in the Brazilian artist's sculptures, but rather a deep, pervasive religious expressionism going far beyond occasional representation of specific *candomblé* spirits. Moreover the syncretism with which both transplanted African religions have accommodated their gods to the gods and saints of official Roman Catholicism enables both Liautaud and Louco to create occasional Christs (fig. 208) and Virgin Marys with a convincing power no longer available to those artists working within the exhausted tradition of Western Christian art.

Behind Louco's *Virgin with Penitent Angels* (fig. 209) one senses simultaneously the emotion appropriate to a Mother of Mankind, compassionately grieving for the sufferings of her children, and the *Mãe de Santo* of *candomblé* sheltering her *filhas* against "possessions" inimical to the welfare of all true believers. But it is the elongated features common to the great tradition of African sculpture and surviving in the long-slumbering Bahian racial memory that give the piece its

206. Candomblé baptismal ceremony at a waterfall near Salvador.

207. Metal staff with candomblé symbols from Salvador da Bahia. Collection the author.

208. Louco, Crucified Christ. Collection Manu Sassoonian.

209. Louco, Virgin with Penitent Angels. Collection the author.

207.

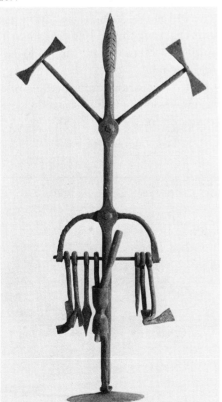

208.

209.

210. Hector Hyppolite, Crucifixion. *Haitian Art Center of New York.*

monumental, unsentimental poise. Hyppolite, the Haitian, had revitalized Christian art with the same "African" sensibility (fig. 210).

Similarly, in such an early Louco sculpture as the *Apostle Seamen* (fig. 211), Louco invests the familiar Christian story of the terrified fishermen on the Sea of Galilee with all the conviction and plastic power

211. Louco, Apostle Seamen. Collection Augusto Rodrigues, Rio.

of the medieval Gothic craftsmen—or of Nacius Joseph (see pp. 133–34). How? In Louco's case by identifying this experience with the experience familiar to humble fishermen on the ocean and rivers of Bahia, and the overall meaning of their miraculous escape from death with the intercession of the *candomblé* spirits invoked by boatmen in Salvador and Cachoeira.

On the other hand, when Louco depicts such a cult spirit directly, as in the image of Iemanja, goddess of the sea, being raised from her watery couch by devoted attendants (fig. 212), the sculptor is drawing, unconsciously no doubt, on the spirit of compassion in Christ's teachings which plays no role in the African cult.

The ingredients of his style that Louco draws from neither religion, but are the inventions of his genius alone, are his use of the concentric rings of the wood (hard jacaranda for the most part) to convey

212. Louco, Sea Goddess (Iemanja) Lifted from Waves. Collection the author.

213. GTO, Triptych, *Church of São Bom Jesús, Divinópolis.*

facial expressions, grief especially, and his splintering to give the effect of streaming hair or breaking waves.

I asked Louco where his present religious beliefs lay. "I belong to all religions," he said. "When I was young I attended many *candomblés,* but I attended Mass too, regularly. Now I am too busy expressing my devotion to the holy spirits through my carvings to attend religious ceremonies. I hope God will forgive me."

"You mean, the gods?"

"Yes," he replied with a serene smile, "the gods."

Leaving, I asked him who the personages were in a blocky sculpture—two large figures above three smaller ones—he was working on.

"Above you have Jesus and his mother. Below are those who betrayed them: a soldier, a policeman, and a lawyer."

In addition to his deeper intuitions, it was clear that the sculptor had a pretty good understanding of this world's political realities.

GTO, Brazil's second major carver of popular art, is also devoutly Christian and a man of the lower middle class, but differs from Louco in being steeped in the Indian cultural heritage of the state of Minas Gerais. Born in a village not far from Aleijadinho's Congonhas, he has lived most of his life in the sleepy town of Divinópolis, a few hours' drive from Belo Horizonte, the *mineiro* capital. "GTO" are the initials of Geraldo Teles de Oliveira, and like Louco he began carving late in life and with no preparation. One of his first carvings, a triptych which he has donated to his parish church (fig. 213), is as perfectly composed and stylistically his own as his latest work.

It was in 1965, when the artist was fifty-two, that he had his first vision. "I had been unemployed at the time," he told me, "and I was desperate. I had never done any carving in my life, not even simple carpentry, but God showed me what to do. My vision showed me a complete piece with all its separate parts, so I had only to go to work. Later I dreamed the chains [fig. 214] that sometimes are linked to figures, but the wheels were my own creativity discovered here at the

214. GTO, Small Figure with Rings. *Collection the author.*

215. GTO, Giant Ring. *Belo Horizonte Museum Art Gift Shop.*

216. *Silhouette of GTO in Divinópolis, holding Ring.*

workbench. I've never stopped working since, except to eat, sleep, and talk to friends like you. I have no recreations—what would I need them for, with all this work to do?"

I studied the three major pieces in GTO's workshop, each a good example of what he makes most frequently. The first, which I will call *GTO No. 1,* was a smaller version of a densely populated "ring" that I had photographed the day before in the Belo Horizonte Museum gift shop (fig. 215). I now photographed the artist holding the smaller piece above his head, or rather his shadow holding it against one of the white adobe walls (fig. 216). What is GTO saying in these rings, whose figures are often so tightly packed inside the circle that some spill over the edges, where they appear to be hanging on for dear life? Is this our spinning earth? Could he be saying that this is where we're at, for better or worse, and that those who refuse to fit in or accommodate themselves to the world's fragile environment will lose their sense of belonging? Or is he saying that the cycle of birth, life, death, endlessly repeats itself and that the only meaning is in the perfection of the patterns? Or—?

The scenario of *GTO No. 2* seems more down to earth. An Indian king or queen presides over the tribe reduced to slavery by the Portuguese colonizer (fig. 217). GTO's grandmother, he had already told me, was an Amazon Indian, seized in a jungle raid by his grandfather, a slave dealer and latter-day *bandeirante* who supplied the mines and farms of Minas Gerais with slave labor. Since slavery was abolished by Emperor Dom Pedro II in 1888, this raid must have taken place almost a hundred years ago. GTO's grandfather died in 1925, the artist told me, at the ripe age of 115. But again, the meaning of the sculpture is elusive, having as little to do with the realities of history in this case as *GTO No. 1* has to do with circus acrobatics. Presumably the "chief" is God for he alone is not chained to his habitat. But why are the ordinary mortals not only chained but given such dimensions that they will fit into their cells only if stuffed or jammed in sideways? The mind of a Gothic painter of the Quattrocento like as Sassetta might *know* what GTO knows, but for us it is only guesswork.

GTO No. 3, the conglomerate with moving parts that doubles as a musical instrument, is the most poetic and mysterious of GTO's creations. He had made several of these *trapizongas,* as he calls them, in the course of his eleven-year career, and we were fortunate in finding one, commissioned and almost finished, in the Divinópolis workshop. Even with a photograph (fig. 218) the piece is difficult to describe. Basically, there are seven upright figures, sixteen inches high—Indians probably, for their headgear is plumed—with hinged arms and legs permitting some movement. They are attached at their backs to vertical rods with cams. These cams are geared to seven pieces of wood protruding from a horizontal camshaft, the shaft itself intricately carved with figures in low relief. When the camshaft, or axle, is rotated by means of two solid wooden wheels, one with a small handle, the seven "Indians" dance up and down, in sequence, not unison, with their hinged arms flapping.

"It's a musical instrument," GTO exclaimed excitedly as he turned the crank to start the seven figures dancing wildly. "It sings the song of the wood with seven distinct notes, all harmonized perfectly . . . you hear it?"

We heard the wood creak, rattle, and shriek, but the "music" was for GTO's ears alone. Could it be a dance of death, a tarantella of devils? Or another symbolic representation of the world, with humanity activated briefly and violently but advancing nowhere?

I asked GTO where he got the idea of this third type of sculpture. From ancient devices, he told me, once used in the gold mines of Minas Gerais to separate the ore from the slag. Was there a connection, I wondered, with Nhō Caboclo's mobiles of gyrating Indians? Could Caboclo have seen one of these mysterious machines on an unexplained visit he'd made to Divinópolis a few years before? Or did their common heritage as Indians lead to similar solutions of making sculpture more lifelike?

Nhō Caboclo—Mister Caboclo, a *caboclo* being a person of mixed Indian and Portuguese descent—was born Manoel Fontoura in the backlands of Pernambuco around 1920 and died in Recife in 1977. The first time I saw him he was lying asleep on a pile of rags on the floor of an unfinished building belonging to Sylvia Martins's Nega Fulô Gallery in Recife. There I had had my introduction to the artist's work the day before: a tiny figure in red and black (Caboclo's austere colors) holding

217. GTO, tribal Indian conglomerate (GTO No. 2) (detail). Collection the artist.

218. GTO with Trapizonga in Divinópolis studio.

219. Nhō Caboclo, O Jabú. Collection the author.

220. Nhō Caboclo whittling a bird at the Nega Fulô Gallery, Recife.

a pole on which has alighted a bird of Pernambuco's far west, O Jabú (fig. 219).

We aroused the artist gently and he sat up rubbing his eyes. He was clothed in rags hardly distinguishable from those he had been sleeping on and one of his arms, deeply scarred from elbow to shoulder, was supported by a dirty sling. He had collided with a car some weeks before, it seemed, and the broken humerus had been badly set. It was the reason, he chuckled, that he had no other sculptures to show us; he said this with an air of having outwitted his taskmasters. He shook an empty whiskey bottle lying beside him to underscore his canniness. But then he picked up a small kitchen knife and winked at me as he began to whittle another bird out of white balsa. Clearly, though he had a ready-made excuse for goofing off and had no intention of surrendering it, he carved instinctively (fig. 220).

Caboclo learned his trade as a boy, hanging around the kiln of Vitalino, a famous folk potter of Caruaru, 150 miles west of Recife; but the rest was all imagination, for unlike Vitalino, Caboclo never repeated himself. The delicate bird with wings slotted and hinged to catch the wind was whittled from balsa; but the painted figure beneath, wound in red and black wool and "armed" with pipe cleaners, was of a harder wood, he told me. So were the multiple figurines of men with saws, in porkpie hats, smoking pipes, and activated by a fan, which someone had commissioned from the Nega Fulô Gallery and which we had photographed there the day before (fig. 221). Where had the sculptor acquired his knowledge of mechanics, his skill in gearing and balancing? Had he, like Calder, studied engineering before his instincts as an artist became dominant? In his case, tinkering with old motors and pumps, perhaps?

He denied it. His principles, he insisted, had been arrived at entirely by experimentation. But surely the old Indian had observed the movements of puppets in the circuses that plied the backland circuits, some activated by cranks or simple clockwork, like the nineteenth-century whirligigs once popular in rural America. One of his sculptures, a mannikin balancing by weighted buckets on a sweep as it rotates on a pinpoint pivot (fig. 222), is a folk toy common to all countries. I had bought one for a few pennies on the dock at Cap Haïtien, Haiti, that year, similar even to the little man's feathered headgear, differing only in the Brazilian's incomparable artistry.

More unique and mysteriously poetic than either these "counterpoises" or the complex assemblages of geared figures are the stabiles which Caboclo called rachos (splits) and which constituted as much as half of his output. Wooden frames of space dividers painted black form the "windows" in which figurines, sometimes painted red and with arms of blackened pipe cleaners, dispute their niches with two-dimensional black birds (fig. 223). Since I had not seen these when I visited the artist in Recife, I was unable to ask him what he had in mind. It is said that he calls these enigmatic homunculi "deads": could the birds be their souls? Could Caboclo be exorcising the demons of the jungle that all Indians of the Amazon region must placate?

Senhora Martins, who had discovered Caboclo idling time away in his native village, brought him to the Pernambucan capital. She

221.

222.

tried to control the sale and pricing of his sculptures in her gallery, but the artist, with as little sense of money as of time, used to sneak out with a piece and sell it in the marketplace for a chicken or a bottle of undistilled rum. Caboclo says he makes sculptures that move because he likes the movies. Why does he like the movies? Because they move! Friends were puzzled over the interminable hours he used to spend visiting a theater that was only twelve blocks away, and at the state of exhaustion in which he returned after his solitary bouts with Hollywood. He explained the procedure to me quite logically. "A bus ticket to the cinema costs 15¢ and entitles me to ride another twenty blocks at no extra cost. Naturally I take advantage of this and walk back to the cinema. On the way home, my return ticket gives me almost two miles additional free ride. No, the bus company isn't fooling Nhō Caboclo!"

Roberto Pontual, the lexicographer of Brazilian art, seemed to confirm the artist's own interpretation of his fascination with things that move. "There is movement implied in even Vitalino's ceramics," he told me, "though there are no movable parts. These artists put movement in their work because they want to catch life, and life moves." Eliane Lage, another Brazilian friend who once ran a gift shop that handled some of the popular sculptors, guessed that Caboclo's use of red in his sculptures symbolizes evil. "The Catholicism of the Northeast teaches an obsession with evil, personified to uneducated peasants, Indians especially, in devil figures colored red and black. When they gave up the innocence of their jungle paradise for Christianity, they received in return fear and the sense of sin."

José Antonio da Silva

The greatest popular painter of Brazil shares with the Indian sculptor two qualities. José Antonio da Silva is as unflaggingly inventive, and his contempt for the opinions of the art world is as absolute. But

221. Nhō Caboclo, Mobile (figures activated by fan). Nega Fulô Gallery, Recife.

222. Nhō Caboclo, Indian (balancing mannikin). Collection Lelia Coelho Frota, Rio.

223. Nhō Caboclo, Racho. Collection the author.

223.

224. *José Antonio da Silva*, Hanging My Critics. *Collection the artist.*

whereas Caboclo's contempt might be ascribed to ignorance or indifference, José Antonio's attitude was acquired over the years as a result of bitter experience.

If Caboclo's subject matter comes out of the dusty attic of the collective subconscious, given visible shape by the toys of itinerant entertainers, José Antonio's imagery reflects one of the world's biggest egos uninhibited by any of the restraints and stratagems that geniuses usually employ to conceal their more outrageous visions. Thus, when sufficiently stung by the patronizing critics of the São Paulo Bienal, José Antonio conjured up a hanging appropriate to their crimes, including in his painting not only their names but a collage of their most impudent reviews (fig. 224). Over the dangling miscreants a sign reads "Divine Justice Never Fails." And pointing out to me the boiling pot to the right, the artist added jocularly: "*That* is where they are going after their bodies are cut down."

Though perhaps not the first of his expressionist pictures, and

225. *José Antonio da Silva*, Landscape with Peasant Farmers. *Museu de São Paulo, Brazil.*

certainly not the best, this painting is important as marking the artist's consciousness of his role as a rebel. The popular "impressionism" of his paintings of the 1940s and early 1950s carried no message, polemical or moral, and offended no one (fig. 225). That was the period of his "discovery" by the critics and collectors of São Paulo, his appearance and award at the Bienal, and his early fame in Brazil at the time when his art and Dos Prazeres's were accepted by the establishment as a kind of Rousseau-like appendix to the works of the Brazilian avant-garde.

Whether José Antonio changed his style because he was goaded by the patronizing attitude of his fair-weather friends, or whether he shifted gears the better to express his turbulent temperament and dislocated life, and therefore lost the avant-garde's esteem, matters little, The far more ambitious and original style on which he then embarked offended almost everyone. By the time I made my first visits to Brazil in 1969 and 1971 José Antonio's pictures were to be seen only in a few déclassé gift shops in São Paulo, and in the budding private collections of such sophisticated naives and militant friends as Iracema Arditi and Crisaldo Morais.

Examples of these are *Stations of the Cross* (plate 50), which José Antonio painted for his local church, and *Sunday Morning,* a good-humored memory of his childhood (fig. 226). In the more daring *Swim-*

226. *José Antonio da Silva,* Sunday Morning. *Collection the author.*

mers and *Crucifixion* (figs. 227, 228) one cannot fail to be struck by an affinity with the paintings of such Middle-European Expressionists of the 1900–14 period as Heckel, Nolde, Kandinsky, and Klee. To imitate such masters (as many have) requires ingenuity, but only genius could achieve similar successes in utter isolation. For like the early Expres-

227.

228.

227. *José Antonio da Silva, Swimmers. Collection Crisaldo de Morais, São Paulo, Brazil.*

228. *José Antonio da Silva, Crucifixion. Collection Crisaldo de Morais, São Paulo, Brazil.*

sionists, José Antonio uses color not to imitate nature but to convey emotion; and his drawing, like theirs, bypasses classic or academic norms to communicate the quintessence of an experience.

Before going to visit him in his home in remote São José do Rio Prêto, I had seen some of these pictures and heard a little about José Antonio's life-style. I had heard that as a young man he whitewashed cemeteries, tamed donkeys, cleaned wells. I had heard that when roses died in his garden he replaced them with plastic buds. I had heard that he played the guitar and watched soap operas on TV. I had read his commentary on the failure of Christianity: "Christ is the greatest, but nobody wants to be Christ." I had enjoyed as much of his autobiography as I could read, and all of the illustrations. I had heard a little about his private life with his wife Rosina and their six children, in the small town ninety miles north of São Paulo, and about his less-private life in São Paulo's Hotel Santa Terezinha with the fabled "Maria Clara" of his second popular novel. And about the war that broke out when Rosina determined to emulate her husband as a famous "primitive" and sold her first picture. (When friends advised the artist that this wifely competition might hurt his prestige and his prices, he destroyed not only her pictures but her brushes and canvases; whereupon Rosina, in a rage, annihilated a series of murals in their home in which her husband had depicted their life together.)

I had also seen a recent painting of his with the disc of a long-playing but slow-selling record he had cut peeping from a slot slashed in the canvas—"so that whoever buys the picture will be forced to buy the record too." (As so often, what would be bad taste in an ordinary talent works for a superior one: the protruding crescent moon of black acetate in this case gives a tree trunk an added dimension.) And I had read in a recent letter a description of the apartment he intends to buy in the metropolis, with a barbecue pit for parties and a library with all the pornographic books and magazines. "I'll pay in *cruzeiros* for the wildest ones," he had added, "but meanwhile I'm like a dry leaf in the wind, or a garden full of beautiful flowers. I live among great joys and great sorrows. Without paint I can't create. But without Maria Clara I can't live."

Expectations aroused by such rhetoric and the slapstick humor of some of the paintings hardly prepare one for the artist's appearance, or the decor of his home. Portly but not fat, sharply dressed, his thick hair dyed black and brushed pompadour-style, he was wearing horn-rim glasses and talking long distance with a client when we came in. Cradling the mouthpiece in his shoulder like any harassed executive (fig. 229), he assured us that he'd be right with us and urged us to make ourselves at home.

What José Antonio says and how he says it quickly dispels this veneer of propriety. Why was he wearing what appeared to be a surgeon's mask in the row of self-portraits that caught my eye? "The critics try to gag me, but I have ways of getting even as you've seen. Besides, I've learned to make use of my gag." He stepped into the small adjoining room where he paints and came out with a rag covering his face below the eyes. "It keeps out the paint pollution—but not *their* pollution!" I looked at the tatters of captioned ribands that swirled about one of these pictures (fig. 230), an expressionist explosion Karel Appel would have approved in which José Antonio sees himself with a Rip Van Winkle beard and wildly popping eyes: *Watch your neuroses! I don't drink or smoke but I adore morenos! Fantasies—the defenses of those being threatened! The capital is full of bullshit; This poor creature is being shot—but he'll shoot back!*, etc.

229. *José Antonio da Silva on the telephone, São José do Rio Prêto, Brazil.*

230. *José Antonio da Silva, Self-Portrait. Collection the artist.*

We walked out into the sun-drenched patio and I showed him a photograph of one of his paintings depicting a séance. "Do you believe in the transmigration of souls?"

"I believe in the wind and the sun, and the rain falling before the sun returns. Everybody has these forces inside him, but few know how to release them—with control. I learned everything by myself, nothing in the thirty days I spent in school. Like all unthinking men, I believed in the Christian gods. But that was in Sallis Oliveira where I was born. Here they taught me science, and the rest I picked up eagerly here and there, until finally the Bienal spoiled me and I forgot everything I'd learned. It was only when I saw they really despised the primitives and were patronizing us for their amusement that I began to learn again what I'd forgotten: that primitive art is pure, like our flag, the color of the Brazilian woods; that the primitive artist's art comes from his heart."

He picked up a guitar and improvised a rhymed song about our visit there to see him. "I taught myself that too, and the violin as well, learning how to compose music and write poems as I went along. You see I grew up among Bahians and Pernambucans. Northeasterners are natural artists, so I learned to create as I sang. An artist must be a poet first—whether he paints pictures or composes music—but I don't need to tell you that. The modern art the critics rave about has lost the poetry. Nothing is left but the bare bones."

Other Painters, Other Ways

In all the history of Brazil, the late Djanira da Mota e Silva was the most famous of painters and the most successful in terms of financial rewards. She was also a *popular artist,* though she had told the press more than once that her work was to be considered in the mainstream of modern art (fig. 231). Visiting her for the second time in her home above imperial Petrópolis, I was reluctant to tell her about a pronouncement made to me by Brazil's leading avant-garde sculptor the week before. The gist of it was that popular art in Brazil was dead. If she agreed, I would be obliged to disagree, and that might be the end of our friendship. But I decided to take the chance . . . did she agree?

Her answer was instantaneous and unqualified. "If I believed that popular art was dead," she replied, "I would be repudiating art itself. I believe in man. I am an optimist. Artists like —— feed on aggression; their work is cruel and grandiloquent. A statement like his is the statement of a primitive human being."

Djanira's art (plate 47) is warm, compassionate, and—whatever she may have borrowed from Cubism in her occasional simplification of mountains and facial planes—deeply rooted in Brazil and its people (fig. 232).

In his book about the Brazilian aboriginals of the Matto Grosso and the Amazon, Claude Levi-Strauss, with that degree of romanticism permitted anthropologists, describes the harmonious life in the

231.

232.

elliptical community dwellings divided down the middle to prevent incestuous breeding, and how the Indians lost that harmony as soon as their Iberian conquerors arrived and resettled them in villages with gridlike plans. Rio de Janeiro was similarly a place of harmonious family living and homogeneous architecture at the turn of the century, if we are to trust the memory of Julio Martins da Silva who began to paint some fifty years later and was still painting with undiminished rapture when I visited that city (fig. 233). There were no automobiles when Julio was a boy, no traffic, no pollution—and no rickety slums, for the village poor had not yet so increased in numbers, thanks to medical and sanitary improvements, that they were obliged to descend on the cities like locusts. And there were gardens dotted with statuary and those miniature "crystal palaces" that Dom Pedro II had admired during his travels to Victorian England and to the Centennial Exposition in Philadelphia (plate 48). The former pastry cook, who had not forgotten how to use glitter effectively, remembered this Rio in the same way that Philomé Obin remembered the Cap Haïtien of the parasoled mulatto élite in their cabriolets driven by black coachmen; or Horace Pippin the drawing rooms of the great ladies of Philadelphia's Main Line.

In one of da Silva's most arresting pictures, Borboleta (fig. 234), a stunning green butterfly has just alighted on the steps of a palace it completely dwarfs. "He's bringing the jungle to a human level," Lelia

231. Djanira da Mota e Silva, Tile Setter. Estate of the artist, Samambaia, Brazil.

232. Djanira da Mota e Silva, Miners. Estate of the artist, Samambaia, Brazil.

233. Julio Martins da Silva at exposition of his paintings in Rio (1976).

234. *Julio Martins da Silva,* Borboleta *(The Butterfly). Private collection.*

Coelho, Julio's discoverer, said to me, "domesticating it." I asked Julio why he had made the insect so large. "To fill the composition." Both explanations made sense. But the old artist was more concerned to give us the scenario of the three tiny girls leaning from the balconies, and the man with the briefcase on the garden path. "He loves the girl above him. The second girl is writing a love letter. But you notice how sad the third girl looks? She wants to be loved but no one loves her."

235. *Fernando V. da Silva,* Bordello No. 2. *Collection the author.*

A much younger black artist of Rio, Fernando V. da Silva, was living on the outskirts of the city at that time, obsessed with the pursuit of love in more fleshly terms. He was (and perhaps still is?) painting bordellos remembered from ports of call up and down the coast while employed as a stoker (plate 51, fig. 235). The humor with which the *carioca* artist conveys these scenes is matched only by José Antonio da Silva—to whom Fernando was not related and whose pictures he had not seen. José Antonio, the poet; Fernando the reporter-cartoonist-dramatist. In the two bordello pictures here, a sociologist of the future might learn more about what life was like in a *boîte de nuit* than he would from a hundred photographs; and he would have a hard time deciding whether the tarts or their clients were having the more fun.

In the frenetic art world of São Paulo, South America's biggest city, talented painters from all over Brazil form a community with considerable esprit de corps. Some, like Neuton Freitas de Andrade, whose pictures seem illuminated in part by the figures' eyes which glow incandescently, are indifferent to modernism (fig. 236). Others, like the late Maria Auxiliadora, "invent" their way into the rarefied ranks of the avant-garde without losing any of their preternatural innocence.

From the outset of her career in 1970, this artist had a very personal style. Perhaps because she had been a housemaid, she painted minutely observed interiors, and nature beyond the windows luxuriating in its freedom. Possibly from this circumstance of her servitude, or

236. Neuton de Andrade, Kite Flyers. Private collection, Brazil.

237. Maria Auxiliadora Silva, Dancer. Private collection, São Paulo.

238. *Maria Auxiliadora Silva, 1935–1974.*

perhaps with an intuition that her life would be short—she was to die of cancer four years later—she sought some means of giving this joyful world an added dimension. And in so doing she invented something new in painting: an undercoat of paint and other substances that would enable portions of the pigment to rise above the picture plane in low relief. Thus, for example, the breasts of her women swell, features are slightly sculptured, and flowers emerge from leaves as though visibly blooming. In the hands of a lesser artist, such a device might have been obtrusive, but in Maria Auxiliadora's freshly disclosed world things bulge naturally because that is their nature.

The dancer in one of her last pictures (fig. 237) is a masterly triumph of impassioned movement over the static fussiness of densely patterned lace.

Gerson de Souza is a self-taught urban surrealist whose fantasies, sexual or mythic, are bizarre but always arresting. His *Blue Crucifixion* (fig. 239) brings the familiar image to life by translating it into the

239. *Gerson de Souza,* Blue Crucifixion. *Collection Oriana MacRae.*

world of magic. Another picture, which I titled perhaps too flippantly *The King and Eye* (plate 49) turned out to be autobiographical, for Gerson wrote me:

A "king" knows everything. He can have people killed. The people kneel at his feet, but he is a prisoner, a solitary being surrounded by people who take care of his life, try his food, watch his bedroom. He does not have the right to love whom he wants. He has no right to privacy. This "king" of mine, however, is a plain man, a man who feels and sees the beauties and mysteries of the world. A poet—a teacher of all the ignored human beings who dream of a better world but have to keep silent, mutilated in their creativity since the days of the cave dwellers. The crown of my "king" is symbolic, all of dream since he is humble and great at the same time. His inner world gives him everything, the music he desires, the colors he wants. He suffers only from the convention that forbids him to talk and live naturally.

The popular artist in Brazil is enraptured by the art of the folk he sees around him, from the painted mud-flap of a truck in the *favelas* (fig. 240) to the feathered dragon of a Bahian ship's prow (fig. 241A). José Barbosa, a young artist of the 1980s, has the power, like Gerson, to

240. *Painting on tailgate mud-flap of truck in Tio favela (1968).*

241A. *Ship-prow carving (1968) in Folk Art Museum, Salvador, Brazil.*

241B. *José Barbosa of Olinda, carved and painted doors. Collection Peter Rosenwald, New York.*

make monuments out of the familiar (fig. 241B). Seeing his doors, and his art, for the first time in New York took me back to Brazil as surely as if a helicopter had dropped me on the boulder-strewn beach at Itapõa.

The popular art of Brazil illustrates two worlds—the mundane and the supernatural—exemplified by these two paintings by Mozinha and Iaponi. Full of feeling and intimate knowledge of their world, they have yet managed to comment upon it. Could Mozinha in his *Wedding at Home* (fig. 242) satirize the rising middle class with such devastating charm if he were *aware* of their pretensions? Probably not. Could Iaponi paint his *St. George Exorcizing a Demon* (fig. 243) were his faith as starry-eyed as those three *favela* maidens who have invoked their cult magician?

The borderline between knowing and feeling is where art begins.

242. Mozinha, Wedding at Home. *Private collection.*

243. Iaponi, St. George Exorcizing a Demon. *Collection Thomas Bridges, New York.*

IV
Indians
Once
Under Spain

*The sense of mystery is important for life, for every-
day living, as it is for love. The sense of discovery, of
adventure, promotes life. Only primitives, or very cul-
tivated people, are concerned with beauty.*
        —Luis Barragán, *Mexican architect*

SINCE IT IS appropriate that Part IV, and indeed this book itself, should conclude with the first "school" of popular artists to emerge outside of Haiti and Brazil, a geographical turn-about is called for and we will consider the Indian artists of Central and South America before taking up Mexico. The folk arts and Indian crafts of Mexico are so much richer and more varied than those of all the other Indian cultures of Latin America that they would deserve to be given a climactic position even if the extraordinary phenomenon of Marcial Camilo Ayala and his Aztec-speaking family in Guerrero had not occurred five years ago.

The *mola*-making Cuna matriarchy of the San Blas Islands will be considered first because it is unique in several respects. It is the only contemporary Indian folk art of Spanish America that has reached its peak in this century, and still flourishes without benefit (as in the case of Mexico's Huichol; see pp. 192–94) of Western guidance. And it is the only tribal art that has managed to assimilate the iconography of alien cultures (or noncultures) without breaking stride or being affected by the utilitarian-commercial purposes of the objects it incorporates.

This aesthetic barrier to outside influences is true to some extent of the embroidered blouses of Indian Guatemala (fig. 244), but the imagery of these descendants of the Mayas has been static for at least a century, and the Indians who still make *huipiles* in a few isolated villages in the northwestern mountain highlands are already being drawn into the guerrilla warfare against an inflexible *ladino* (mixed-blood) regime—a conflict that seems likely to end with the Indians' extinction or total acculturation.

Isolated popular artists of great talent, like António Velásquez in Honduras (fig. 245) and the late Asília Guillén in Nicaragua, have painted without issue. An attempt by the Catholic-Marxist poet Ernesto Cardenal to establish a colony of peasant painters on an island in Lake Nicaragua (plate 61, fig. 246) came to an end when the civil war of 1979 caused the evacuation of the island. Whether this promising ex-

1
Introduction

244. Indians in traditional costumes in the village of Nahualá, Guatemala.

246. Chael, Fishing Village, Lake Nicaragua. Collection the author.

245. António Velásquez with painting, Tegucigalpa, Honduras (1970).

247. *Noé León, Priest and Jaguar. Collection Alvaro Cepeda Samudio, Barranquilla, Colombia.*

248. *Mario Tulio Villalobos, Benediction. Collection Daniel Storper, New York.*

periment will be revived now that Cardenal has become minister of culture in the Marxist government that ousted the Somozas remains to be seen.

A few popular painters, of whom Noé León (fig. 247) and Mario Tulio Villalobos (plate 58, fig. 248) are the best known, exist in Colombia, where folk tradition except for an isolated potter or two is almost extinct. But in Ecuador and Peru, where tribal crafts and the remnants of the Inca culture still flourish in mountain fastnesses and jungles, popular painting has begun to come to life. From Bolivia, where the descendants of the Incas also survive marginally, come woven coca bags, alpine hats, *totora* (balsa-reed) boats, and the fantastic Lucifer costume still worn at Corpus Christi devil dances along the shores of Lake Titicaca (fig. 249).

In Chile, where the Araucanian Indians put up a legendary war-to-the-death against the conquerors, little or nothing in the way of folk art survives. The Incas with their rich culture barely reached Chile, whose culture since the Conquest has been almost as Europeanized as Argentina's. An exception was Violetta Parra, a sister of the mathematician-poet Nicanor Parra. Perhaps Violetta, a folk singer, was inspired by the same passion for the folk that animated her friend Pablo Neruda, Chile's great poet. In any event she succeeded single-handedly in almost filling the visual vacuum. Her yarn paintings—had she heard of the Huichol far to the north in Mexico's San Luis Potosí? (see pp. 192–94)—dealt for the most part with the folklore of Chile's history. The one I was lucky enough to photograph at an exhibit commemorating Violetta's recent death, which I attended with Neruda in 1969, depicts a stirring incident in the War of the Pacific (1879–83) between Chile and Peru (fig. 250).

249. *António Viscara Morales and Francisco Maydana Morales, Lucifer mask and devil-dance costume.*

250. *Violetta Parra, Incident in the War of the Pacific. Yarn painting.*

2

The *Mola*-Makers of Panama

251. Mola. From Parker and Neal, Molas.

252. Cuna Indian Woman. From Parker and Neal, Molas.

NO ONE KNOWS exactly how or when the *mola*—that wonderful two-panel blouse with designs in reverse appliqué—originated. A hundred years ago it didn't exist, and only in the 1920s and 1930s did it begin to assume its all-encompassing ingenuity. But since there is historical evidence that the Cunas, long before they migrated to their present home on the 365 San Blas Islands, painted their faces and bodies in brilliant colors, the likeliest theory is that, once clothed, the Cunas found a way of perpetuating their art in the less perishable *mola* (fig. 251).

An English traveler, Lionel Wafer, gave a revealing description of the body-painting of the mainland Cunas in 1699. "They make figures of birds, beasts, trees or the like . . . but the figures are not extraordinary like what they represent, and are of different dimensions as their fancies lead them." The women, he added, "are the painters, and take great delight in it. The colors they like to use most are red, yellow, and blue, very bright and lovely." But it wasn't until more than two centuries later, when the Cunas had moved to the islands and acquired needles, scissors, and thread, that two English women, Lady Richmond Brown and F. A. Mitchell Wedges, visited the San Blas archipelago in 1922 and acquired the first collection of what they called "hieroglyphic cloths," sixteen hundred of which (mostly abstract) are now in the British Museum.

No one knows where the Cunas originally came from. The theory is that they migrated from Southeast Asia in the fourth millennium B.C. and that some of the visual symbols in their picture-writing may be traced to Mesopotamia and predynastic Egypt. Another theory, based on no more than the Cunas' visual resemblance to the Mayas (short, big-shouldered, tiny-footed), has it that they migrated from southern Guatemala. There is evidence that they did cross the mountains to the coastal slope in the sixteenth century, which may account for the fact that the men still do their agriculture and draw their water on a narrow reservation on the mainland. But there is no evidence that they settled in the island chain until about 1850. Earlier, the Spaniards had attempted to subdue the Cunas without success. The Colombians were no more successful. Following Panama's declaration of independence from Colombia in 1904, half-hearted attempts to integrate the Cunas were made. In 1925 the Cunas proclaimed the independent Republic of Tule whose flag was a blue swastika in a field of orange with a red border, but neither the flag nor the republic caught on, and in 1938 an agreement was made between the Panamanian National Assembly and the Cunas under which a resident Panamanian governor on Porvenir Island recognized the right of the local caciques to maintain law and order throughout the islands. The three caciques are paid by Panama to do so—a charter of virtual autonomy which works, so far, very well for all concerned.

Since the Cunas have never had a written language, their religion and myths are transmitted orally, by song, and in the pictures of the *molas*. The Cuna model of the universe is Dantesque, with sixteen layers aside from the earth's, eight for heaven and eight for hell. The disembodied spirits can be hostile, and the Cunas huddle together for protection against them. Medicine men (shamans) offer protection, and so do tiny carved wooden idols (*uchus*), medicinal herbs, and the fumes of hot peppers.

Despite fertility symbolism in the traditional *molas,* sex is the only taboo in subject matter. Sexual intercourse is forbidden in the island lodgings and a marriage can be dissolved if the groom jumps out of the bridal hammock more than once. If he does, of course, he stands to lose everything because this is a matriarchal society with all property vested in female hands and the *molas*—now a greater source of income than the traditional coconut—are created by women only. The male, whose responsibilities are mainly to fish and till the mainland farms, is indeed a drudge in Cuna society—and a drab drudge (fig. 253) with his conventional shirt and slacks, compared to these peacock-queens with their golden noserings and breastplates, bracelets and anklets of orange beads, facial stripes, and above all—*molas!* Though predominantly red, the *mola* may contain as many as twelve colors, so intricately revealed through their "windows" and embroidered (for such tiny details as a cat's whiskers or a TV's fine-tuning knobs) as to defy analysis. The earliest *molas* seem to have been the most abstract, though possibly what seems abstract to us may have been pregnant with meaning to those who made and wore them. Then came the *molas* enriched by and enriching legendary or religious experience (plate 53). And finally the *molas* of topical or political content picturing everything from an elephant's bath (fig. 254)—"There are things easier to understand than the reason for such an animal," said a Cuna at her first circus—to advertisements turned into images bordering on the sublime.

I first visited the San Blas Islands with Bill Negron in 1965 when nothing had been written about the Cunas and the *molas* were being

253. Cuna couple. From Parker and Neal, Molas.

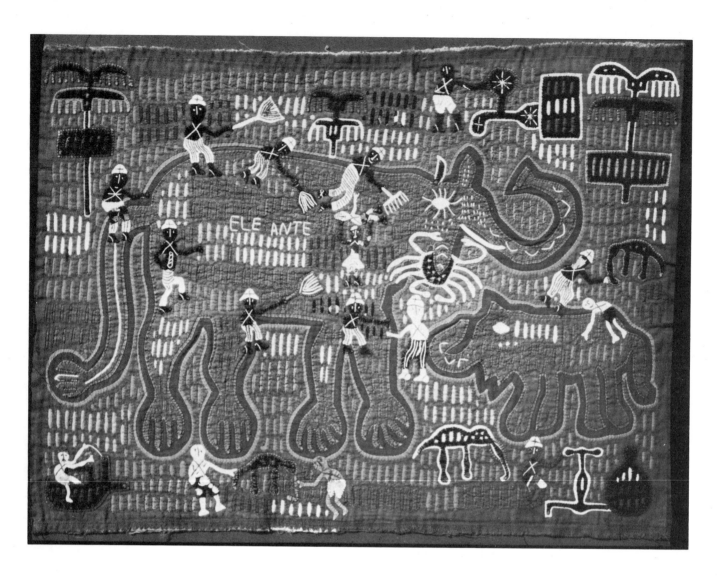

254. *Elephant-bath mola. From Parker and Neal,* Molas.

bought mainly by a handful of Peace Corpsmen from Panama proper. The women were suspicious at first (fig. 255) but became very friendly when we let them use our cameras, inviting us to eat and drink *chicha* with them. Even then "acculturation *molas*" were predominant; for ever since work on the Canal began and the men worked there for good wages, shoulder patches, sewing machines, bicycles, electric fans, circus animals, and the like had become part of the iconography. We noticed that in the *molas* imitating political election posters, the lettering of the slogans was jumbled—an appropriation of language for its visual interest alone. We noticed also that the Cunas were still close enough to nature to see beauty in fleas, rats, armadillos, crabs, snakes, and other creatures considered repellent by us; and that when they appropriated record-album covers or TV sets surmounted by penguins, they transformed these commercial images into works of art (figs. 256A, B).

Much has been written since about the *molas,* and perhaps definitively by Ann Parker and Avon Neal, whose book is not only a visual delight but a model of sympathetic perception. They point out, for example, that when the space capsule was appropriated (plate 54), the Cunas, far from acknowledging that men had actually traveled to the

255. Three mola-wearing Cunas, Panama
(1965).

256A and 256B. Penguin TV ad and mola
derived from it. From Parker and Neal, Molas.

257. Mola, *Petertubo village.* From Parker and Neal, Molas.

moon and back, were simply making use of what they considered an amusing fable; for subsequent *molas* continued to depict the *real* explanation of a lunar eclipse: the attempt on the part of the jaguar to devour the moon, an act which must be prevented by sending an albino with bow and arrow to the rooftop to shoot the beast down. (There are more albinos, incidentally, in the San Blas Islands than anywhere else in the world. Exclusive intermarriage among the twenty thousand Cunas accounts for this. Albinos are not allowed to have sex, the males being dressed in women's clothes and permitted to sew *molas*—as close a passport to paradise as Cunaland can offer.)

Parker and Neal are not sanguine about the survival of this great art. The Cunas are allowing hotels to be built on some of the islands and inferior *molas* almost mass-produced are now sold in the international airport in Panama City and are exported for cushion covers. But while it lasts, they point out, we can expect a few more of the best and the brightest. "The collective genius," they conclude, "contradicts everything that we in the West have glorified in our cult of the individual. . . . The Cunas maintain a continuing style, a homogeneity of vision and visual effects . . . never concerned with who did which mola . . . their joy of expression and sense of humor always at their fingertips."

3
Guatemalans and Other Central American Image Makers

258. *Hardware-shop sign in Chichicastenango, Guatemala.*

Every group or town has its own dress, woven by its people, usually on the primitive hip or stick loom, with the traditional symbolism of their history and ancient gods forming the pattern. If you should pass a man or woman on the roadside as you hurtle by in your car, you will be able to tell what town they come from, and often, by the way she has her skirt wound round her, whether the woman is married, and whether the man has children, and what standing he has among his own people.

—CARMEN L. PETTERSEN

WHEN I SPENT the winter of 1965 in Guatemala, visiting every part of the country, the individuality Carmen Pettersen describes still existed, although only in certain isolated Indian villages was the weaving still unadulterated and not for sale. The *zut*, an embroidered man's headcloth such as the one I acquired in Nahualá, is probably no longer made (plate 55). Nahualá in the time of General Ubico resisted acculturation fiercely, insisting that it run its own school and refusing to permit the sale of liquor; it paid Ubico annually the equivalent of the liquor tax to gain this privilege. *Huipiles* like the one I collected in the remote highland village of Nebaj a few years later may still be made there. It represented a year's work—and was sold at the asking price only after a day's pleading (plate 56).

259. *Bargaining for a zut, Nahualá, Guatemala (1965).*

261. *Indians burning pagan copal at Catholic church, Chichicastenango.*

260. *Maya Indian wearing a huipil, Nebaj, Guatemala (1970).*

At that time the major Indian ceremonial centers of Chichicastenango and Momostenango were already overrun by tourists, but their Indians were clinging stubbornly to their local rites, blankets, and *huipiles*, though these were being sold in quantity on the streets of the capital, products by that time without innovative variations. A few other villages like Zuníl, Sololá, Cobán, Sacapulas, San Pedro Sacatepéquez, Todos Santos Cuchamatán, and the tiny settlements in the shadow of the volcanoes at the western end of Lake Atitlán were still populated by Indians with distinctive dress and shamanistic rituals.

The Maya-Quiché, most populous of all Middle American Indians and still to be found in Mexico's Yucatán, are most numerous and culturally most intact in the highlands of Guatemala. The Maya-Quiché practice of tie-dying—cotton or silk so tightly bound before dipping that only the parts exposed take color—exists elsewhere only in India and on the island of Bali. Its practice here long predated the Conquest though no examples survive from that time, except as they are depicted in Maya sculpture and mural painting (fig. 262A). I was told in Guatemala that Alvarado, Cortez's able and ruthless lieutenant who conquered Guatemala and whose moustachioed mask is still worn in fiestas at Chichicastenango (fig. 262B), decreed that each village retain its distinctive costume undeviatingly, as a precaution against rebellion; but I have never been able to corroborate this. Middle America was the only part of the two continents where a hieroglyphic writing developed, and this is a component of the surviving imagery although the meaning of the language has long since been forgotten.

Another factor accounting for the survival of so much for so long—but also virtually guaranteeing its imminent destruction—has been the fact that Guatemala's ruling class, unlike Mexico's, has always regarded the Indians as inferiors. The Mayas' hatred for their

262A. Maya mural at Tikal (restored). National Archaeological Museum, Guatemala City.

262B. Angel Gonzalez. Moros (Alvarado masks), Comalapa. Collection the author.

oppressors has been as strong, of course, and innumerable violent uprisings have occurred, all of them going without mention in the controlled press of the rulers. (Note the sullen but subservient expressions of the Indians between the Alvarado masks in Angel Gonzales's painting.) As recently as 1944 a false rumor that the Mayas were rising in

263. Andres Curuchic, Funeral Procession.

revolt led to the massacre of every *ladino* in Patzicía, an outburst that had to be quelled by government troops and caused the fall of the Ponce regime.

Popular painting has developed in Guatemala, but only sporadically, and most of it to satisfy a tourist demand for souvenirs more durable than embroideries. Popular sculpture has never developed beyond folk sculpture (plate 57). The oldest of the painters, Andres Curuchic, was born in 1897 in Comolapa, from which most of the other painters also came. An Indian of the Cakchiquel branch of the Mayas, Curuchic paints weddings, baptisms, funerals, wakes, and gatherings

264. Margarita Chex, Musicians. *Collection the author.*

around the village fountain, sombre in hue, realistic in intent (fig. 263). Santiago Tuctuc of the same village is almost as well known, arranging his carefully garbed Indians against tiled, whitewashed buildings. Others in the Comolapa group include Curuchic's son, Santiago, Angel Gonzales, Ivan Gabriel and the Chex couple, Julian and Margarita (fig. 264). Of all the Guatemalan popular artists, only Miguel Achpacaja has a style going a bit beyond documentary realism. He paints penitents, marimba players, processions, and *combites* (work gangs) in a field with a disdain for perspective that relates him to the classic Maya. Achpacaja's wood panels with floral frames (fig. 265) may be more

265. Miguel Achpacaja, Bailán Combite. *Putumayo Gallery, New York.*

BAILAN COMBITE

closely related, however, to the bark painters of central Mexico, whose art will be discussed later.

In Costa Rica, Joaquín Chaverri of Sarchi still paints carts as his father and great-grandfather did before him, with a dazzling geometry of colors that would make any Op painter envious (fig. 266).

Painters with more accomplished styles but related much less distinctly to the folk tradition in their countries are José António Velásquez of Honduras and the late Asília Guillén in Nicaragua. Velásquez has one subject only, his native village of San António de Oriente with its pretty little white church surrounded by tile-roof buildings and a sprinkling of people and animals (fig. 267). The magic of this subject, considered from various angles, is in Velásquez's sure compositional judgment and in the brushwork that gives trees and flowers a furry richness contrasting nicely with the stark white-walled cottages separated by cobbled streets. Guillén (1887–1969), an embroi-

266. *Joaquin Chaverri, painted cart. Sarchi, Costa Rica.*

derer by profession who took up painting late in life when afflicted with arthritis, uses the same tiny brush strokes as Velásquez with an effect as magical but with more variety of subjects. Her use of minuscule figures, identical in size whether in the foreground or on a distant mountainside, is surely related to her precisely detailed needlework.

267. *António Velásquez, View of San António de Oriente (1965).*

THE PRE-COLUMBIAN CULTURE of the Incas had reached its peak, perhaps started to degenerate a bit, when Pizarro and his band of 126 intrepid cutthroats landed at Tumbes in 1532. It was the last and artistically the least inventive of the series of cultures that had flourished along the spine of the Andes for several millennia. The culture of Chavin de Huantar had originated in what is now northern Peru and had produced a sculpture as pure and majestic as that of the forebears of the Indians of the Northwest Coast. Further to the south in the lands surrounding Lake Titicaca, the culture of Tiahuanaco had left monumental reliefs glorifying the jaguar-god. The embroidered mantles of Paracas, perfectly preserved in the dry heat of the desert to the west of Tiahuanaco, are as fine as any ever made. Later, in the centuries immediately preceding the Inca conquest of the Andes, coastal cultures, the Chimu and the Mochica, flourished, the latter perfecting a realistic style of pottery, biographical, anecdotic, erotic. And still farther to the north, in what is now Colombia, monumental stone figures appeared; and later at the other extreme, miniature figurines in gold exquisitely cast in the *cire perdue* process, related to the work of pre-Columbian craftsmen in Costa Rica and Panama but having nothing at all to do with the Chimus, Mochicas, and Incas to the south.

The artistry of the Colombian Indians, yielding to the Spaniards' insatiable greed for gold, died at the source. The talent but not the tradition is evidenced in the pottery of Raquirá (fig. 268) and in the work of such isolated painters as Mario Tulio Villalobos in Cali and Noé León in Barranquilla (see fig. 247). But one has to proceed further south, into Ecuador, to find living folk arts with a continuous line of descent and enough vitality to be mutating into forms new and strange.

Ecuador

The Incas did conquer Ecuador just before Pizarro's coming but not with enough force to impose their Peruvian patterns on the culture already there. The Quechua spoken by most highland Indians was not discouraged by the Spanish missionaries. Surviving folk arts indigenous to Ecuador include the wool devil masks of Imbabura: the painted transformation masks in wood and leather from Cotopaxi; the bread-dough figurines from Pichincha province; the horned-deer headdresses of Chimborazo; the polychromed ceramics and *vacas locas* (mad cows) of Pujili (Cotopaxi); the plaited basketry and straw figurines of coastal Montecristi and the Amazon jungle; the painted balsa birds and traditional jungle ceramics of San Jacinto of Sarayacu; the painted drums of Cotopaxi and the skin-paintings that have emerged from them; and the rugs and textiles of Riobamba, Otavalo, and Cuenca.

The woolen devil masks are of a startling originality equaled only by the devil masks of Puno (see plate 52). They are worn at the fiesta of San Juan in the province of Imbabura. The wearer is temporarily in

268. Pottery with reliefs. Raquirá, Colombia (1970).

269. *Wool devil mask of Imbabura, Ecuador. Collection the author.*

270. *Ceramic vessel from Sarayacu, Ecuador. Collection Olga Fisch, Quito, Ecuador.*

league with the *huma* to acquire his fighting power. The mouth and eyes are embroidered with fretwork; the nose and ears protrude like handles; and the fearsome "hair" is wired to stand up straight, like Medusa's serpent-locks (fig. 269). The wood and leather masks worn by the *disfrazados* (disguised ones) at fiestas in Cotopaxi give their wearers attributes of monkeys, birds, and other beasts; they resemble similar transformation masks in Mexico, Guatemala, and Panama.

Sculptures made out of bread dough, painted and shellacked, are found in Ecuador only. Originally from Carapungo (Pichincha), they were made to be eaten on the Day of the Dead or left on graves. Now manufactured in Calderon, gaudily painted and varnished, they are a popular tourist item all over Ecuador.

The ceramic ware of the jungle Indians from San Jacinto of Sarayacu (Pastaza, fig. 270) seems (and is) closely related to the abstractly painted pottery of the Shipibo tribe in Peruvian Amazonia (fig. 271). The women of the Canelos Quichua originally made this exquisite painted pottery to serve *chicha* (manioc- or premasticated-corn beer of low alcoholic content, a staple food to the Canelas, drunk to secure harmony within the household). The steps by which the pots are made, decorated with stone-derived paints, and coated with *shinquilla* (a tree resin) are related in fascinating detail by Norman Whitten in his *Sacha Runa*. In abbreviated form:

No temper is used. Coil by coil the pot is built up. Then the woman kneads the piece into the exact form desired, striving for thinness of sides and ample dimensions. . . . She nips around the rim, closing it with lips and teeth but leaving no mark. When dry, a new slip, *allpa,* is added. Then comes the polishing with the female soul stone, first of three souls imparted to insure that the woman's ability and soul substance shall live on. . . . The design is another amalgam of general female knowledge and special secret knowhow, acquired from either the artist's mother or her husband's mother. . . . As she applies the black and red stone colors, the artist "thinks" special songs. . . . She uses her own hair as brush; then bakes; then glazes with tree resin. The figurines portray tree mushrooms, the moon, the jiluca bird or anything that has captured attention recently from a jukebox, a Mexican wrestler or an insect. . . . Finally the piece is fired over a low flame, buried in hot ashes and then rubbed over with resin again.

When Olga Fisch, the Hungarian refugee artist and folk-craft dealer, who stands in relation to popular art in Ecuador as DeWitt Peters to Haiti, first visited these jungle artists she convinced them that it would be profitable to turn out pieces of maximum quality more frequently than once or twice a year. She also became concerned about the men. It had been bad enough to play no part in the religious-creative affairs of the tribe; now the women were making all the money too! She talked with a committee of men and they came up with an unexpected art of their own: carving jungle birds and other animals out of balsa wood and painting them in brilliant colors (fig. 272).

Señora Fisch's role in the development of Ecuadorian popular

271.

272.

painting was crucial. An art of painting the skins of ceremonial drums existed among the Salazaca Indians of Cotopaxi province. The adult males in the village of Tigua were already busy painting their drums when Olga persuaded the younger boys in the Toaquiza Vega and Ugsha families to cut the lamb- or goat-skins in squares or oblong shapes instead of circles and to stretch them by nailing them to solid frames—frames which could also be painted to "complete" the picture just as the painting of the circular drumhead had extended into the frame and cylindrical barrel of the drum. The boys thought that would be "fun," Olga told me; and they've been making as much money as their fathers ever since. Their paintings are Ecuador's first excursion into popular art that goes a little beyond tribal craftsmanship (plate 60, fig. 273).

Painting in the Latin-American mainstream is of course produced

271. *Shipibo potters with ceramic vessel, Pucallpa, Peru.*

272. *Painted wooden birds. Collection Olga Fisch, Quito, Ecuador.*

273. Fiesta. *Painting on goatskin, Cotopaxi, Ecuador. Collection Robert Brady, Cuernavaca, Mexico.*

274. Oswaldo Guyasamín, painting. Museo Guayasamín, Quito, Ecuador.

in Quito, but more so than any other such art it seeks to relate itself closely to the folk tradition. Most famous of these painters is Oswaldo Guayasamín, who is old enough to have been influenced, when he was residing in Mexico in the forties, by the styles of both José Clemente Orozco and Diego Rivera and also to have acquired a measure of Diego's idiosyncratic Marxism. Like both Mexicans he turned against not only the ruling class in Ecuador (whose three hundred families of European extraction then owned sixty-five percent of the arable land, selling their *huasipungeros* [peasant serfs] along with the fields when the land changed hands) but also against the Catholic Church. ("Even the dogs go to church in Quito," Ludwig Bemelmans once remarked.)

Guayasamín's mosaic murals in the presidential palace show the Spanish conquistadores in 1533 on their way to discovering the Amazon after destroying the Inca Empire and imposing a regime far more brutal on Ecuador's Indians. The artist's recent work, more influenced by Picasso and less obtrusively Marxist (fig. 274), is seen to best advantage in the private museum this enterprising artist has established in the capital.

Other sophisticated Ecuadorian painters almost as renowned are Eduardo Kingman, of the same generation, and Oswaldo Viteri, now in his late forties. Kingman's painting reflects the trials of the *huasipungeros* indirectly, sometimes through their hands alone—"the hands of the soul" as one viewer called them.

Viteri's dependence on peasant inspiration is much more oblique. In his recent paintings he glues multicolored rag dolls, bought in the market, in circular or square masses to create very large, essentially abstract, canvases (fig. 275).

275. Oswaldo Viteri, painting. Collection the artist, Quito.

Peru

The automobile, the radio and cheap factory products are accomplishing in a few years what the Spanish failed to do in 300 years—destroy the heritage of the people.

—ROBERT EBERSOLE

Robert Ebersole's lament is more true of Peru and Bolivia than it is of Ecuador, although he takes no account of the efforts of folklorists and artists to give the dying traditions new life. Twelve years ago when I visited the villages of the *altiplano* from Huancayo and Cuzco to the shores of Lake Titicaca and on into Bolivia as far as Cochabamba and Potosí, the folk arts were relatively alive and well. The engraved gourds (*matés*) of Huancayo were an art that had changed very little from pre-Columbian times (fig. 276), and this was still so when I revisited Peru in the fall of 1980. But in nearby Ayacucho and Quinua I found almost nothing of the superb ceramic religious sculpture that was flourishing in 1966 (fig. 277); and the astonishing *retablos* (altarpieces), one of which I photographed that year with its creator, Hector

277. Ceramic sculpture from Quinua (Ayacucho), Peru.

276.

Guzman (fig. 278), were being turned out now only in small models for the tourist trade in Lima.

The first known *matés* date from 2000 B.C. and they have been found all over Peru. The modern inheritors of the tradition live in the villages of Huantas and Cochas Alta close to Huancayo in the Andes.

276. Matés. Engraved gourds from Huancayo, Peru (1968). Collection the author.

278. Hector Guzman and his wife with retablo, Ayacucho, Peru.

278.

279. Indian blanket of llama wool depicting astronaut, Altiplano, Peru. Collection the author.

One variety is scorched, then engraved with red-hot pointed sticks, and finally burnished. Depending on the temperature of these tools, a broad range of brown tones from very light to black is obtainable. A black soot from burnt *ichu* (mountain grass) is then rubbed over the surface of the calabash, blackening the light-colored lines. Oil is then rubbed into the surface.

Transition from the "old style" gourds to a new brown-on-beige variety featuring contemporary peasants playing musical instruments, tending llamas, fighting bulls, and so on is attributed to Isaiah Zagar, a Peace Corps volunteer stationed in Cochas in the mid-sixties. Types of engraved gourds still used as musical instruments all over Peru are the elongated fish-shaped gourd (*guiro*), notched and stroked with a comb, and the common bottle-shaped "cha-cha."

Two other folk arts deserve mention. One is the blanket of llama wool made by the Indians of the *altiplano* (fig. 279) who sometimes incorporate spacemen and other incomprehensible phenomena of modern technology into the spirit world of animals with as much ease as do the *mola*-makers of Panama (see pp. 170–74).

The other folk art, perhaps made in southern Peru but most often in Bolivia, is the devil dance costume (plate 52) worn during the Corpus Christi dances in the villages fringing Lake Titicaca on the border of the two countries. The chest plate and apron panels are made of woven grass mats covered with satin and set with glass stones, imitation pearls, and embroidery. The belt consists of old coins. But the mask, with its globular glass insect eyes, mirrored fangs, and studded horns framing a fiendish phoenix, is perhaps derived from the Indians' terror at encountering the helmeted conquistadores for the first time and is as awesome as anything in the whole range of folk art.

Popular painting in Peru has come into its own in the past year or two among artists of the *altiplano* who use brilliant but subtly contrasting colors on wood panels. They come from the isolated village of Sarhua in the high Andes, accessible only by mule or on foot and virtually untouched by "civilization." The two most consistent painters are Victor Yucra and Primitivo Evanon Poma.

Hinchaway (*Putting the Roof On* in Quechua, plate 59) is captioned by Evanon Poma as follows:

> When a house is finished, the owners, godparents and relatives will go round the house, with great pleasure and deep satisfaction, dancing to the music of horns and drums. . . . One wears the costume of a legendary figure. Another is a majordomo in charge of the liquor. There is also a dance master and priest. Ichu grass is being carried, along with beans, to complete the roof. After the dance there will be a ceremony presided over by the kinfolk honoring Pachamone, the earth mother who has sheltered them in this world, and the Apusuyo [gods of the mountain].

Adulterio (*Adultery*), unsigned, (fig. 280), is captioned as follows:

> Adultery is forbidden. Any man or woman caught at it will be punished by the authorities by being made to walk through the

280. Unsigned, Adultery. From Sarhua, Peru. Collection James Segreto.

281. Celestina Villalba, Fiesta. Collection James Segreto.

town streets with horns on the head, and then fastened in the stocks where they will be whipped.

These artists have been encouraged and exhibited by Bernardo Luck and Juana Tornawiecki of the Huamanqaqa gallery in Lima, which also exhibits exclusively another talented popular painter, Celestina Villalba of Jauja near Huancayo. Her painting illustrated here (fig. 281) depicts a fiesta honoring a hero of the 1879 war with Chile.

As in Ecuador, the honesty and strength of popular art has begun to find recruits among those artists of the establishment who are bored with the predictability of formalism. The most successful of these rebels, thus far, is Victor Delfin.

Born in 1927 near Piura in the north, Delfin, one of eight children, began working for his blacksmith father while still a boy, grinding bits for the oil rigs. At Paita on Sundays Victor and his brothers watched other Indian children catching fish and made hooks of their own from the spent shell casings at the local army firing range. "We stole enough string from the fishermen's nets," Delfin told me, "to make our own lines. We used sacks of cartridges for weight, and caught enough *meros* and *corvinos* from dockside to feed the family and sell to neighbors too!"

At eight the ingenious boy drew well enough to "instruct" in the Piura school. At fourteen he won a scholarship to art school in Lima, but it didn't pay enough to feed him during vacations. "Even now I can't stand the summer months because I think back to those vacations when I almost starved to death." After eight years of this, Victor was eligible for a scholarship "abroad." Most of the students were pulling strings to go to Paris or Rome but Victor, already in love with Peruvian folk art, chose Ayacucho. "There I learned what art is all about. I saw so-called folk artists, the despised 'primitives,' creating masterpieces. I learned from them to use my hands again as I had in Piura. I learned to *make* things, using imagination too. They threw me out of the art school finally on charges of immorality. The immorality was loving the popular artists and being willing to learn from them and make my students study their work. I went home to Piura, where my father was polishing the drills, and had my first show there. With the money from selling fifty paintings and sculptures, I went to Chile. I introduced myself to Neruda's friend, the famous painter Nemesio Antunes. He said to me, 'You don't need to introduce yourself. You're the troublemaker from Ayacucho who loves popular art!' He arranged exhibits of my work, and another out of the trunkful of folk ceramics from Ayacucho I'd brought with me. Both shows sold out. So I was able to go back to Lima with enough reputation to receive commissions."

Delfin's creative energy is the equal of Morrisseau's, but his ability

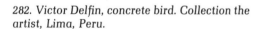

282. Victor Delfin, concrete bird. Collection the artist, Lima, Peru.

to put this energy to work in convincing forms wholly his own is inconsistent. A concrete dove on a Brancusi-like pedestal in his garden is truly monumental (fig. 282). His bronze horses and metal birds exude power. The forged, intricately embossed cast-iron stove he has made for himself (and others) with its firebox breathing flame from a devil's mouth is still more impressive (fig. 283). But such a commercial commission as the fountain in the lobby of the Sheraton looks like something thrown together by an interior decorator: metal columns supporting metal butterflies, angels, and demons lit from the inside through "stained glass windows" made of old bottles. In painting, too, Delfin's taste falters when a project gets too big or too ambitious to control. Portraits and religious scenes work well, but a series of copulating horses professing to illustrate Neruda's *Veinte Poemas de Amor* would surely make the spirit of the poet wince.

The moral, if there is a moral, is that artists who deliberately subject themselves to the rigors of popular art re-enter the world of the avant-garde at their peril. To play the game of the intellectuals one must be an intellectual—or a force elemental enough to induce among critics the fear of being left behind. Until the Delfins of the art world are sure enough of what they want to say to say it unequivocally, they will be left in the no-man's-land between those who create because they feel themselves a part of nature and those who keep the home fires of modern art safely burning.

283. *Victor Delfin, iron mask. Collection the artist, Lima, Peru.*

5
Mexico

284B.

284A.

285.

284A. Candy skulls, Toluca, Mexico (1957).

284B. String-animated calaveras, Mexico. Collection Olga Fisch, Quito, Ecuador.

285. Pre-Columbian skull frieze at Chichén-Itzá, Yucatán, Mexico.

BOOKS HAVE BEEN WRITTEN, and will continue to be written, about the folk arts of Mexico. And none will ever be definitive. From the face-painting of Sonora and the glazed ceramic animals of Tonalá, the painted plates of Pátzcuaro and the inlaid trays of Uruapán, the polychrome figurines of Metepec and the angel-studded candelabra of Acatlán, the regal blankets of Toluca and the embroidered blouses of Oaxaca and Yucatán, from the anthropomorphic water jars of Tehuantepec to the tasselled saucer-hats and black *huipiles* of Chamula, the subject is inexhaustible.

Two lines of provenance are constant. The older, the Maya-Aztec-Toltec heritage, runs down the spine of Mexico, from the Indian villages north of Guanajuato and San Miguel Allende south through Yucatán to the Guatemala border, where of course the Maya component begins to predominate.

The candy skulls and string-animated *Calaveras* (skeletons, figs. 284A, B), still sold in every Christmas stall from Acapulco to Vera Cruz, are domesticated grandchildren of the fearsome pre-Columbian reliefs (fig. 285). The *voladores* of Papantla and Cuetzálen "flew" around their maypoles as weightlessly a thousand years ago as they do today. The Olmec *tigres* around the baptismal font at Yecapixtla roamed the jungles to the east long before the Toltecs came north in pre-Aztec times. When Padre Sahagun accompanied the conquistadores to Mexico he recorded the undying animism of his Indian converts:

Haciendole acontesido à la Niña Hermelinda Rodriguez vecina de l... de ...... el dia 1.º de Mayo de 1882, alarses dos enfermedade peligrosas invocaron sus Padres à Nuestra Señra. de los Dolores del Calvario de ...... y al Sor. del Prendimiento de San Felipe quedando buena y sana, por lo que dan gracias à Divina providencia por tan portentoso milagro.

When we die
We don't really die
Because we are alive: we come back to life,
We go on living, we wake
And this makes us happy.

286. Retablo, Mexico.

287. Acrobats. Painted ceramic assemblies from Acatlán, Mexico. Collection Olga Fisch, Quito, Ecuador.

The second great component of Mexican folk art had already begun to flourish and from the onset accommodated the existing traditions rather than creating a complete break with the past. The Virgin of Guadalupe, Mexico's most powerful Catholic symbol, was envisioned with an Indian face in 1531 by the Indian Juan Diego and so she has survived to this day. The Christmas-Eve *piñatas* and *retablos* painted on tin or wood to commemorate at the altar some miraculous escape or cure, are mainly Spanish Catholic in descent but with Indian overtones (fig. 286). The acrobatic *angelitos* of Acatlán (fig. 287) and the guitar-playing mermaids of Metepec (fig. 288) are hybrids too—piety with a pagan wink.

The most isolated Indian tribes of Mexico—excepting only the Lacandones of the deep forests of Chiapas who never came in contact with Spanish-speaking Mexico at all—are the seminomadic Huichol of the Sierra Madre Occidental and the Nahuatl-speaking Aztecs of Central Mexico, most especially those in the mountain valleys of Guerrero inaccessible by road. Not surprisingly, these are the people who have created the purest, most inventive folk arts in Mexico (plate 62), and,

288.

288. Mermaid. *Painted ceramic from Metepec, Mexico. Collection Olga Fisch, Quito, Ecuador.*

289. Mermaid *(detail) from Guerrero, Mexico. Polychrome wood. Courtesy Ron Podell, Cuernavaca, Mexico.*

289.

more surprisingly, the only folk arts that have expanded into popular arts (fig. 289).

The Huichol: Rediscovering the Tribal Soul—in Yarn

To the primitive man religion is a personal matter, not merely an institution, as with most Christians, and therefore his life is one continuous devotion to his deities.

Religious feeling pervades the thoughts of the Huichol so completely that every bit of decoration he puts on the most trivial of his everyday garments or utensils is a request for some benefit, a prayer for protection against evil, or an expression of adoration of some deity. In other words, the people always carry their prayers and devotional sentiments with them in visible form.
—CARL LUMHOLZ, Unknown Mexico, 1902

Until the last decade or two (when the Mexican government started using helicopters), the Huichol in their roadless chasms west of San Luis Potosí were out of reach—as they wanted to be. Their traditional crafts were still oriented to drawing the attention of the ancestor-gods to the maker and his family. These crafts included woolen belts and *bolsas* (shoulder bags) woven with seemingly abstract designs, gourd bowls for fertility, ceremonial plumed arrows, and the so-called god's eyes used in a wide variety of animal symbols in yarn work (fig. 290).

On my second visit to Mexico, in 1956, I bought a woven belt and bag after a very long search. Returning ten years later, I saw the "god's eyes"—much more perfunctory ones than the example here—for the first time in a tourist shop in Monterrey. They were being turned out in quantity and I assumed that that was the end of Huichol art.

I was wrong. In the last decade, encouraged by Juan Negrin, son of the last premier of the second Spanish republic, young educated Huichols in Guadalajara and other cities along the Pacific slope have returned to their tribal villages. There they have undergone the arduous rituals involved in becoming shamans, and now they are interpreting the myths in yarn paintings of extraordinary complexity (plate 63).

Before discussing these works of art and their principal creator, José Benítez Sánchez, a word about the Huichol religion may be helpful.

The Huichol tribe, related to both the Nahuatl-speaking Toltecs and Aztecs and to the American Hopi (see pp. 47–50), originated in what is now the state of San Luis Potosí, where it successfully resisted both the Spaniards and the Franciscan missionaries. The seminomadic Huichols, gradually driven west into the Sierra, began to focus their ancestor-worship on pilgrimages. One such was the pilgrimage to the Pacific to ask for rain. But more important was the annual trek to the desert land in the northeast, in search of the peyote they took as a sacrament and to hunt deer, the supreme sacrifice to the deities in nature.

As in all post-Columbian Mexican Indian cultures there is a certain amount of syncretism involved, but much less than with most: the Divine Mother in the Huichol religion is closer to Coatlicue than to Mary. The Christian God is venerated under the name of Tatata Ampa. And all the images of the saints—Christ and the Virgin included—are symbolically buried on Good Friday, to be resurrected with the sacrifices of a bull as the sun rises. Copulation is taboo during the month-long search for the mind-bending peyote buds, and is punished by everlasting torment if practiced with non-Huichols.

The key religious symbol of the Huichol, the *nierika*—the "god's eye" in its degenerate form—is actually an instrument (the Aztec's "smoking mirror" of Tezcatlipoca?) for seeing the invisible, conjuring up the sacred ancestors, and protecting the faithful against the evil eye.

It was probably the traditional method of making these *nierikas*—described by Lumholz a century ago as involving yarn and beeswax—that led to the contemporary yarn-painting in both its commercial and authentically innovative varieties. For it is this technique, the "abstract" symbolism of the woven bags and ceremonial face-painting (fig. 291), and the *nierika*—"like an opening into the supernatural world, a channel through which the Ancestors may enter into man's reality"—that gave José Benítez Sánchez and his fellow shaman-artists their key to a new art.

Sánchez was born of pure Huichol stock in Wautua in 1938. At the age of eight he started to be trained as a shaman by his adoptive father. He recalls the ceremonial deer hunt in which he came upon the small animal in a rope trap (these traps are called *nierikas* too), held its snout in his mouth until it expired, and then underwent penance: six years

290. *Insects with "god's eyes." Yarn painting from San Luis Potosí, Mexico. Collection Olga Fisch, Quito, Ecuador.*

291. *Huichol Indian with face-paint, parrot-feather cape, and woven belts. Rancho Las Huntas, Nayarit (1937).*

292. José Benítez Sánchez, Dream-Visions at the Edge of Darkness. Courtesy Juan Negrin.

without sex or salted food. At fourteen the boy went to the coast and became (psychologically) a *mestizo*. He learned Spanish and worked for the government. In 1963 he made his first yarn paintings. In 1968 he was invited to perform Huichol dances and music at the Olympic Games. Three years later he left the government service, where he was being forced into the distasteful role of a critic of his own people's art, and began to devote himself exclusively to interpreting religious truths through his paintings. In tribute to the inspiration that came from his most vivid dreams, he wrote: "Nierika is a Peyote" and thereafter assimilated effortlessly into his art even such "alien" elements as the San Francisco Bay area, the Berkeley hills, and the plane which brought him on a visit from Mexico (fig. 292).

Tutukila Carrillo, who was born in 1949, began making commercial yarn paintings in 1963. After returning to the ancestral homeland for spiritual sustenance, he began to create serious work in serial form. Negrin distinguishes his art from Benítez Sánchez's as "more reflective and style-conscious."

Marcial Camilo Ayala and His "Aztec" Family

> *Ecstasy is identity with all existence ... the apprehension of the infinite in every moment.*
> —PETER MATTHIESSEN, The Snow Leopard

One day in the year 1977 Marcial Camilo Ayala, a descendant of the Aztecs who lives in a remote mountain hamlet in the Mexican state of Guerrero, was painting a picture. Twenty-six years old, he had been an artist for five years. That picture was the first to be quite detached

293. *Marcial Camilo Ayala,* Our Village. *Collection the author.*

from the "bark" tradition of his village and the painted ceramics for which the whole Xalitla-Ameyaltepec-San Juan district is noted. Little more than a year before, Marcial had painted a "realistic" summing-up of the village's life: a very large picture with more than seventy figures, glowing (as all the pictures by his family would soon glow) with a primordial harmony long gone from this world, but enclosed, as though protectively, in a double band of "bark" arabesques (fig. 293).

There were no floral borders in the painting that followed. The scene is of night, and in the star-studded sky a crescent moon is ringed with a black halo. In the left foreground an immense throng of Indian penitents in sable robes seems to be celebrating the Day of the Dead. But what they are carrying proves, on closer inspection, to be not the usual coffin but a crêche. The crowd holds aloft a Nativity, illuminated by a blaze of light from one of the thatched huts. The wax candle which each peasant carries serves, cumulatively, to illuminate from within a tree dominating the center of the picture like a transparent green lantern. The candles carried by the crowd as it approaches the horizon merge with the stars. Nature and man are one (plate 64, fig. 294).

Where in the world we inhabit is the scene of this painting by Marcial Camilo Ayala to be found? Where, for that matter, was the execution depicted six years after the event in Goya's *Third May 1808* to be found? Or the beggars on crutches in Brueghel's *The Blind Leading the Blind?* Everywhere and nowhere. Everywhere in the sense that anyone who had ever witnessed man's inhumanity to man, or the degradation imposed by poverty and disease, could witness the truth of these statements. Nowhere in the sense that whatever these artists

294. *Marcial Camilo Ayala,* Nocturnal Fiesta. *Collection the author.*

might once have seen had been sublimated in the artistry. Marcial was among those contemporary painters, like the ones we have visited in Haiti and Brazil, who are concerned to convey information about their place and time, and at the same time to say something about it without preaching. Would a visit to the actual scene of this living artist's *Nocturnal Fiesta* reveal how an artist transforms reality?

I was thinking along these lines as I left the highway linking Acapulco and Cuernavaca. At a pretty roadside town with a little blue-domed church, the mountain track fords a shallow stream, winding its way around boulders, higher and higher. The dust was almost suffocating. Four years before, the first outsiders to penetrate to the artist's village hadn't found any road at all, and they had been greeted with fear. Now, waving to the peasants on their burros with a friendly "Ahtay!" ("good morning" in Nahuatl), those pioneers were guiding us into the village. As we climbed up and down the eroded *barrancas* (ravines), thinly clothed in mesquite, thorn, and organ-cactus, highly stratified outcroppings seemed to indicate the passage of a giant river millions of years ago. Trees hung precariously by their exposed roots on this awesome terrain. Vistas of isolated volcanic peaks punctuated the horizon. Here and there morning glories and golden-eyed Susans clustered in shady spots. Finally we drove through a dry riverbed, past cairns of boulders to a gate in a barbed wire fence that marked the village.

It nestles dustily above the Río Balsas, broad, swift, shallow, brown, the banks dotted here and there by peasant women clubbing their laundry on the pebbly shingle. The houses are of mud brick, hairy with straw from the manure used to cure them. A few have tile roofs, but most are thatched, with ceramic pots along the ridge-poles to let the smoke out. Poorer houses, as in Haiti and Brazil, are wattled (fig. 295).

Marcial, broadfaced, high-cheekboned, with eyes as "Oriental" as an Indonesian's, came out to greet us. He has a lovely smile, the kind that masks no secrets. He had built this house for his father, who now stepped through the door, followed by Marcial's brother, Felix Camilo. Marcial was building his own home of stone on the village's perimeter overlooking the river. As our eyes became accustomed to the half-light inside the Ayalas' house, we saw an altar at the far end; behind it a small pergola with artificial flowers. Chromos of the saints stood on the altar, each with its votive candle in a glass. On one of the makeshift beds a fat book was lying, *Encyclopedia Universo*. A tape player on a table was surrounded by recordings of Beethovan, Mozart, Dvořák. On another altar stood an unfinished painting by brother Felix, a pair of Tretorn tennis shoes hanging over it by the laces. Piles of long black beans in one corner, broken painted urns in another. Marcial's mother was busy making small ceramic deer and angels. A young girl offered us newly baked bread in the shape of a mermaid. Other artists in the family joined us as we continued talking.

Ten years ago, Marcial said, no one ever left these villages. Now many of the men do. He himself has visited Acapulco and Mexico City. But painting, he was soon to say, "has become my way of looking into my past, my people's past."

295. *Typical dwelling in the Ayalas' village (1979).*

I had with me a photograph of the painting of the transcendental night procession. I showed it to Marcial and asked him if he remembered painting it. He did indeed. And he pointed out the actual street from which his celebrants disappear into the velvet night. "But where is the tree?" I asked him. "The miraculous tree of light." Smiling and tapping his forehead, the artist answered: "I had one here. I suppose I'd seen it somewhere, sometime. When the picture called for it, there it was."

Everywhere and nowhere.

Background

Almost a thousand years before the Italian Renaissance, the art of painting was highly developed in Mexico. Giles Healey's 1946 discovery, deep in the Lacandon Forest of Chiapas, of Mayan murals in a hidden temple encrusted with a protective limestone deposit, only confirmed what had long been suspected: that painting, whether on walls, ceramics, or statuary, was a pre-Columbian art as highly developed as architecture and sculpture (fig. 296B).

During the centuries of the Conquest and Spanish colonial rule, the arts languished in Mexico. Excepting ecclesiastical architecture,

296A. *(Left to right) Inoséncio, Roberto, Carolyn and Edmond Rabkin, Marcial, Felix Jiménez, the author. Guerrero (1979).*

creativity of any kind was discouraged. It was conducive, the authorities believed, to a dangerous independence of mind. But in building the great churches and monasteries, the bishops fell back perforce on the craftsmanship of the enslaved Indians. The beautiful church carvings of wood and stone were all executed by Indians. But painters from the nation that had produced Velásquez and Goya had not been encouraged to visit or emigrate to the New World. And if reproductions of Hispanic masterpieces, a rarity even in Europe, ever reached Mexico, there is no evidence of it.

The astonishing eruption of mural painting that followed the Mexican Revolution of 1913–23 has been ascribed to the release of Indian creativity, but there is little evidence for that. None of the major artists were Indians, and while *zapatismo* had given considerable romantic prestige to the traditionally exploited Indian majority, Indian types and their picturesque clothing and customs were superimposed on styles already firmly grounded in the provincial academy or the European avant-garde of 1910–20. The paintings produced in Paris during that decade by the young Diego Rivera were Cubist in inspiration. An Italian trip to investigate mural techniques of the early Renaissance contributed a bit more to the narrative pictorial style that Rivera began to develop in the twenties, and which he used to cover the walls of the Ministry of Education in Mexico City with his powerful, quasi-Marxist celebrations of indigenous virtue.

The more hard-headed José Clemente Orozco, meanwhile, was creating a very personal style (fig. 297). It derived in part from classical Roman and Renaissance wall painting and in part from exposure to the satirical brilliance of José Guadalupe Posada, a popular engraver of the pre-Revolutionary decade whose political demonology had obvi-

296B. Procession. *Bonampak mural (c.* A.D. *730–820).*

297. José Clemente Orozco, Migration. *Fresco. Dartmouth College Library, Hanover, N.H.*

296B. 297.

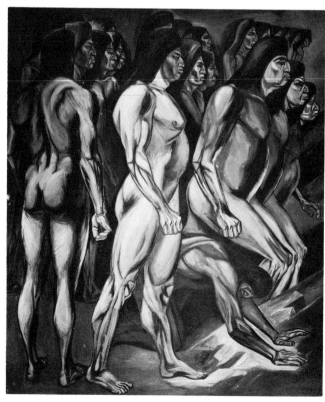

298. *José Guadalupe Posada, Boss Politico as a Serpent. Engraved cartoon (c. 1910).*

ous folk antecedents (fig. 298). The youngest member of the mural triumvirate, David Alfaro Siqueiros, more impatient than Orozco but just as ambitious, adapted European expressionism to his particular Marxist overview of the newly discovered Aztec "heroes."

The decades of Mexican easel painting that followed in the wake of the mural renaissance exploited the vein of *indigenismo* less obviously. Francisco Goítia had been the first to mine it with his smoky mysticism of the tragic poor burning their devotional candles in dark corners. Rufino Tamayo, of Zapotec origin himself, presented familiar folk types whose symbolism he explored with the aid of Picassoesque distortions.

At no point, as styles became more sophisticated and less Mexican, was there any sign of the popular painting that might have been expected, and which was already developing in African Haiti and Afro-Indian Brazil. Folk arts flourished, as we have noted, as nowhere else in the hemisphere. But until Miguel Covarrubias and Donald Cordry began to collect them in the thirties, the polychrome wood and

299. *Devil Riding Dragon. Folkart of Guerrero. Early twentieth century. Collection author.*

199

hammered metal transformation masks from inaccessible, roadless Guerrero and other "backward" states were a high art known only among connoisseurs (plate 62; fig. 299). It would be convenient to establish connections between the genius of these exorcists of evil, many of whom thrived in the villages to the south and west of the Ayalas', and the source of Marcial's inspiration, but actually his painting had its immediate roots in a local tradition less ferocious and inventive. For decades, the Ayalas' village had been the fountainhead of a ceramic pottery painted in earth-reds on a cream slip and decorated with mythical fauna and flora of the most benign sort. Simultaneously, bark painting closely related to this pottery and depicting scenes of village life was being made by these same craftsmen on paper bought from the Otomi Indians of San Pablito in the state of Hidalgo.

Paper makers to the Aztec priesthood, the Otomis had continued the practice throughout the post-Conquest centuries—no longer to leave records, for Montezuma's libraries had long since been burned by the barbarous Spaniards—but for magic. The craft of the Otomis is an intricate one. Once the *brujo* (sorcerer) has cut the *amatl* paper from the tree, it is imbued with magical properties and no scraps are left lest they serve as counter-magic. White paper represents the good; gray and russet sheets, evil.

At the beginning of this century the paper was still made in Tepoztlan, not far from Cuernavaca in Morelos, which adjoins Guerrero, but today the Otomis of distant San Pablito exercise a monopoly. Their white paper is made from the inner bark of the fig or mulberry. Strips five feet long are peeled from the trees and rolled into bundles. The women then soak the bark to remove the latex sap, discarding the outer skin. Under the new moon, the inner bark, now dry, is boiled in limewater left from cooking corn. When soft and pliable, the damp paper is placed on flat wooden boards and beaten with hand-size lava stones. Once dry, two leaves of paper are annealed.

Villagers from remote Guerrero could now bargain for the essential raw material on which to paint their familiar arabesques and scenes of village life, hawking them later on among the tourists of Cuernavaca, Taxco, and Iguala.

Seminal Encounter: The Family

One day late in 1972, walking through the main square (*zocalo*) of Cuernavaca, Edmond and Carolyn Rabkin, a young American couple who then owned a successful New York shop featuring exotic costumes, were accosted by a young Indian with a bundle of bark paintings. His "barks" (fig. 300) were hardly better than others the Rabkins had seen, but something about the Indian with his open, friendly smile was compelling. They invited the young painter to visit them in their home; and since he spoke a few words of Spanish they also asked him where he came from and whether he'd like to try his hand at less conventional scenes should they provide him with oils, acrylics, and sheets of Masonite.

He introduced himself as Marcial Camilo Ayala. He was twenty-one years of age. His village lay several hours off the main highway

300.

300. *Marcial Camilo Ayala, bark painting (1972). Collection Edmond and Carolyn Rabkin, Cuernavaca.*

301. *Muñecas (painted ceramic figures). Collection Robert Brady, Cuernavaca, Mexico.*

302. *Marcial Camilo Ayala, Self-Portrait. Collection Galeria Lara, Cuernavaca, Mexico.*

303. *Marcial Camilo Ayala, Market. Early painting with floral (bark) style. Collection James Segreto.*

301.

connecting Cuernavaca with Mexico City and Acapulco. This village, accessible only by muleback, or in good weather by a four-wheel drive truck, was one of many in Guerrero effectively isolated from Mexico's Hispanic culture. Twelve years before, living in Cuernavaca for some months, I had been intrigued by the gaily painted *muñecas* (large ceramic figures) which these villagers sold at a roadside stand south of Iguala. I had bought some. Robert Brady, the well-known tapestry maker who lives in one of the Cortez palaces in Cuernavaca, already had a collection of them. I had photographed and reproduced them in my book *The Mexico Traveler* (fig. 301). In one of his early pictures, Marcial uses the evolution of his art—from ceramic artisan to bark painter to full-fledged artist—as the background for his self-portrait in peasant garb (plate 66, fig. 302).

Under the sympathetic eyes of the Rabkins, who had now moved permanently to Cuernavaca, Marcial and his family began to paint systematically (fig. 303). Two of Marcial's brothers, Felix and Juan, were the next to paint in styles of their own. But at first Felix had so much trouble that the Rabkins consulted Marcial about him. Marcial offered to talk to Felix. The two brothers returned to their village for a couple of weeks. When they returned to the Rabkins' compound in Cuernavaca, the two Americans were astonished by the high quality of Felix's new pictures. "What did you say to Felix?" they asked Marcial. "I said to him, this is our great opportunity to express ourselves: to paint honestly whatever is in our minds, or before our eyes, or in our hearts."

Felix began to paint church processions and moonlit scenes of village life. There were caravans of donkeys bearing the painted urns to

302.

303.

304. *Felix Camilo Ayala,* Country and City. *MIND Collection, Norwalk, Conn.*

305. *Juan Camilo Ayala,* Procession to the Mountain. *Collection Dr. and Mrs. Lloyd Siegel.*

market; interiors of the thatched hut illuminated by starlight; a pastoral scene of villagers washing their clothes in the Río Balsas, preparing their nets, eating slices of melon, with only a spiky distant view of metropolitan Mexico as a reminder of civilization and its discontents (fig. 304). The starlight in many of these pictures, Felix explained to me, has to do with the time when they are painted: daylight hours are devoted to agriculture.

In a self-portrait almost as masterful as Marcial's, Felix depicts himself, brush in hand, as though conducting a symphony over a painting, which lies upside-down on the table in front of him. The idea came to him, he explained, when he noticed the reflection of himself on the glazed table top. But the upside-down painting-within-a-painting, he added, never existed except here. He put it in as an afterthought. The figure to the right is his father. I asked him about the face in the moon. "The moon has a personality. So does the sun. The jars on the windowsill behind me contain Liquatex."

Juan Camilo's poetic paintings often depict fiestas (fig. 305). In an early one with an elaborate bark-painting border, gaily costumed celebrants crowd the foreground. In the more distant middle ground, blue and mauve volcanic peaks lift out of the arid table-land beyond a winding river. Above hover protecting angels in white. The sun benignly gazes at the antics of the revelers with an expression at once amused and tragic (plate 65).

Cousins of the three Ayalas, and themselves brothers, are Felix and Inoséncio Jiménez Chino. Inoséncio's brush drawings in Chinese ink are beautifully adapted to conveying the poetic rhythms of village life. But on occasion Inoséncio has painted moonlit landscapes with overtones of violence and magic. In one such picture, bandits skulk in the shadows of rocks, preparing to waylay the villagers on one of their distant *milpas* (fig. 306). In other pictures Inoséncio conveys pity for the poverty of less fortunate Indians.

Felix Jiménez, on the other hand, is attracted by very complex schema, bringing together segments of his life and dreams enclosed in

306. *Inoséncio Jiménez Chino,* Bandits Threatening Our Milpa. *Private collection.*

flowing "windows." In one such picture, painted for the Rabkins, the artist's relations with his patrons unfold like still-frames in a moving picture. Each "cameo" is enclosed in a profile "portrait" of the Rabkins and connected to a central cameo: a portrait of the artist as a child in a pear-shaped "womb." Asked why he portrayed himself there wearing a fancy star-studded shirt but no pants, Felix answered quite seriously that a shirt was all his family could afford to clothe him in at that time. Rabkin and his daughter Lara are the central figures in the lower right quarter. "What are they doing?" I asked. "Helping the poor." They are depicted inside the artist's profile. Carolyn Rabkin, elegantly dressed, is shown in an adjoining "window" inside her own upside-down face. In still another, the artist as a child is shown "dreaming" under the protective hand of his father. "We all go through these cycles from birth to death," Felix Jiménez sums up. But everything is painted by free association.

Felix Jiménez now rivals Marcial himself in his ability to conceptualize without becoming didactic. In *The Lovers* (plate 67, fig. 307) of late 1979, two young people, holding hands, "dream" with their eyes wide open. Above them floats a dark sphere enclosing—so subtly as to be almost invisible—their unborn child. The negative space in which dream and dreamers are suspended is shaped into apelike profiles benignly kissing the swollen circle of the young girl's pregnancy.

307. *Felix Jiménez Chino,* Lovers. *Collection the author.*

Sixth and last of the painters, distantly related to the other five, is Roberto Maurício, whose distinctive style cannot be confused with theirs. His sense of fantasy is highly developed, and he conveys it in muted colors with a draftsmanship of great sensitivity.

In one recent picture, a woman's shawl in a heap occupies the foreground; above and a little to one side a woman's profile observes it—the profile of a very white woman. A tear is falling from the "eye" of the shawl. Artist's title: *The lady has lost her shawl and the shawl is weeping for the lady.* A barbed satire on the possessive obsessions of the white middle class? Surely without any conscious intent.

One of Roberto's most poetic pictures, *The Witch,* involves a

308. *Roberto Mauricio, The Witch. MIND Collection, Norwalk, Conn.*

309. *Roberto Mauricio, Discovery of My Girl. Drawing in ink with painted background. Private collection.*

nightmare the artist had in which he was pursued through a moonlit landscape of lacy black trees by an airborne *bruja* (sorceress, fig. 308). In a Chinese-ink drawing of the year before, the artist, mounted on a burro as spiritedly as any medieval knight on his white charger, has surprised a lovely *muchacha* washing her clothes in the Rio Balsas. The scene is revealed on what appears to be a placemat; the frayed border with its thousands of threads must be touched to convince the viewer that it is indeed painted (fig. 309).

Marcial

The art of Marcial differs from that of his brothers and cousins not so much in quality as in content. Roberto's paintings and Juan Camilo's are as poetic, Felix Camilo's as bold, Felix Jiménez's as original.

What sets Marcial's art apart from theirs is his soaring imagination, the daring with which he invents ways of projecting new vision after new vision. It would be accurate to call Marcial's art highly sophisticated were it not that the connotation of "sophistication" has come to imply an awareness of the high art of the period. Marcial's is rather the sophistication of a Brancusi who emerged full-blown from the folk traditions of his native Rumania, and in Paris by a process of refinement and reduction came up with "abstract" archetypes. Marcial could say with Brancusi, "My life has been a succession of marvelous events," or "I give you pure joy," but he could not say as the great sculptor did, "When we are no longer like children, we are dead." That *consciousness* of the virtue of the childlikeness implies an awareness of the corruption of sophistication which has no place in Marcial's world—as yet, anyway. Marcial does what he does, not to make a point, but because it expresses most directly and accurately what he feels.

His "openness" is by no means confined to painting. Encouraged by Edmond Rabkin, he taught himself Spanish with the aid of a Nahuatl-Spanish dictionary, using as his reader the Spanish version of Castaneda's *The Teachings of Don Juan,* which the American thought would appeal to his mystical nature. At the same time, Marcial was mastering the guitar, and acquiring tapes of some of the classical composers for the battery-operated tape player which he had bought in Cuernavaca and taken to the village. When he told me that Beethoven was his favorite composer, I found a tape of the *Eroica* at a music store in Cuernavaca and presented it to him. He listened ecstatically to the great symphony on the Rabkins' powerful hi-fi. "That's precisely the music I heard on the radio a year ago, my introduction to Beethoven. I've been listening vainly for it ever since. How did you know?"

In the *Self-Portrait* of 1976 Marcial, in peasant garb with broad-brimmed sombrero, gazes solemnly at the viewer as if to say "Here I am at this point in time," but it would be wrong to assume that humor has no part in his personality. He is amused by his father who used to chide him for wasting his time painting but who now, with unprecedented wealth rolling in, adjures him to "Paint faster, son! Paint faster!" When Rabkin once asked Marcial whether there were prostitutes in the village, he answered with a smile, "Not enough." A much later portrait, the luminous *Old Man in Thought* of 1981, is an almost mystical journey into the borderline between life and death (fig. 310).

There is no apparent distinction in Marcial's mind between representation and abstraction. Just as there is no sense (our sense) of time as an absolute. In an early picture, *Preparation of Corn,* the space is divided into three parts, each with its own suns and moons to combine the cultivation of two days and a night within one frame; and the artist's pictorial logic is irresistible. A still earlier (1975) "abstraction" of concentric circles and dots turns out to be Marcial's image of his own eye, taking in the miracle of his expanding awareness (fig. 311). In *The Dream* of 1976 (fig. 312) a *culebra* (snake) is pursuing the artist. "Only from behind is it a snake," he told me. "In front it's a woman. It will never reach me because I am flying." In the still earlier *Fiesta en la Vida,* the festival of August 28 is shown taking place simultaneously

310. *Marcial Camilo Ayala,* Old Man in Thought *(1981). Jay Johnson Gallery, New York.*

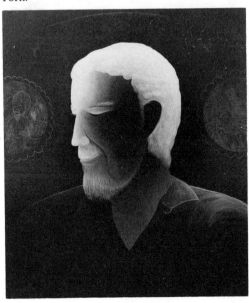

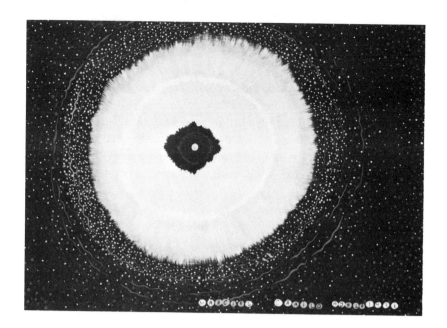

311. *Marcial Camilo Ayala,* The Artist's Eye *(1975). Private collection.*

312. *Marcial Camilo Ayala,* The Dream *(1976). Private collection.*

on earth and in the sky. "As a child," Marcial explained to me, "I once heard music coming from the sky. *'Arriba!'*" he added, pointing up, "but no more."

"You don't need it any more, Marcial, you have Beethoven."

"When I heard Beethoven for the first time, I recognized the music. It was the same I'd heard so many times coming from the sky!"

The almost frightening force of such a recent picture by Marcial as *Mother and Child* (see fig. B., Introduction) derives in part from the daring distortion of the child's face, staring up at the mother from the *rebozo* which holds it to her neck; in part from the generalized purity of the monumental profile. The resemblance to some of Picasso's neo-classical Amazons of the 1920s is coincidental. This is no bravura tour de force abstracted from hundreds of hours spent contemplating archaic fragments in the museums of Spain, France, and Italy. Marcial's painting grew out of his musings on a mother's devotion. The spray of blossoms with the golden butterfly serves to relate the human image to nature. If that image is impersonal, that is because the artist wished that particular mother to stand for all mothers—just as Picasso's more knowing genius managed to transform his Graeco-Roman prototypes into timeless evocations of the modern ballet.

Equally compelling, and more unprecedented in its originality, is *The Wave* (plate 68, fig. 313) of the same year (1979). Never has energy been conveyed more directly. As the wave surges toward the spectator from a vanishing point on the horizon between two low verdant cliffs, its raw power is defined by three human figures. One plunges headfirst into the torrent. A second precariously rides the crest. The doomed third is visible only as an underwater shadow. The wave crests in such a way that its whitecaps look like gulls about to take off into the sky which alone promises salvation. Marcial told me that he had been thinking about the Río Balsas since childhood. Where did it come from? Whither was it going? The picture reflects this mystery, the mystery of life itself.

Other recent ambitious paintings deal more obliquely with Marcial's interpretation of the world he knows. Some are simple celebrations. One, *Walk through the Seasons,* anticipates the renewal of life through a springlike, verdant "window" in a serene, autumnal panorama. *A Dream of Times Past and Present* is a wide-angle perspective of whirlwinds and volcanoes enclosed by the artist's hands and feet in the four corners with his flattened face at the top. "Our valley was once under water," Marcial says, and this geologic sense of time is reflected more succinctly in the *Tilted Landscape* of 1979 whose layers of stratified rock enclose precious stones and a gray ancestral profile (fig. 314).

Earlier that year Marcial had still been naive enough to regard the projected electrification of the Balsas Valley as an unmixed blessing. Looking with him at his small *Electricity Comes to Our Village* in Cuernavaca (fig. 315), I had been reminded of a passage in Yukio Mishima's novel about a similarly isolated community of unspoiled, beautiful people:

> The village was suddenly ablaze with brilliant lights. It was exactly like the opening of some spectacular, soundless festival: every window shone with a bright and indomitable light without the slightest resemblance to the smoky light of oil lamps. It was as if the village had been restored to life and come floating up out of the black night. The electric generator, so long out of order, had been repaired.

313. Marcial with The Wave *(see plate 68) (1979).*

314. Marcial Camilo Ayala, Tilted Landscape. *MIND Collection, Norwalk, Conn.*

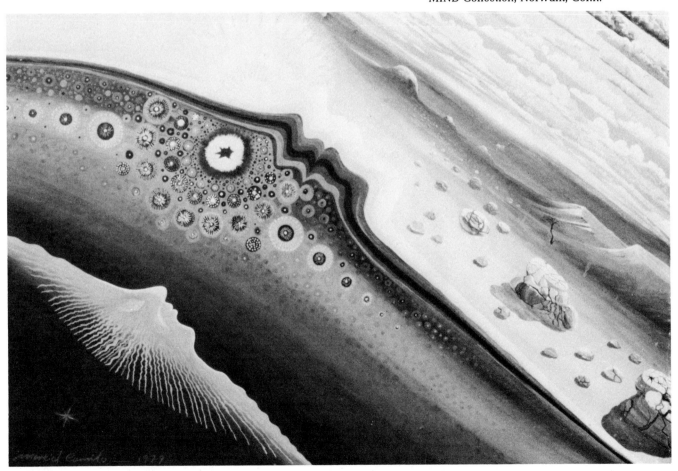

315. *Marcial with* Electricity Comes to Our Village *(1979).*

But early in 1980 Marcial painted a picture which must have been suggested, unconsciously perhaps, by overheard conversations about the doom toward which Mexico and the rest of the world seems to be sliding. Marcial now rendered his beloved valley in gradations of gray alone. The arid surface of *What the Sun Sees* is populated only by graves, crosses, abandoned tools and weapons, ghosts (plate 69). The once-verdant terrain with its industrious peasants survives only as an after-image in the sun's "eye" (detail, fig. 316)—contained there, Marcial seems to be saying, forever, but never to be reborn on this ungrateful planet.

The worlds of the popular artists, Marcial's included, are serene worlds; and if permitted to survive this terrible century, their visions of order and harmony will provide mankind with the only real alternatives to alienation and despair. Whether conceived on the shores of Bali or the mountains of Montenegro, the snows of Yakutat or the burning sands of Namibia, their message will always be the same: give us the freedom to create and we will rediscover the nobility of the past, make gods of men, and conceive a future worthy of the nature that put us here.

316. *Marcial Camilo Ayala,* What the Sun Sees *(detail). (See plate 69). Collection the author.*

Bibliography

PART I

American Indian Art: Form & Tradition. New York: E. P. Dutton, 1972.

Ashton, Robert and Stuart, Jozefa. *Images of American Indian Art.* New York: Walker & Co., 1977.

Baker Lake 1977 Prints/Estampes. TriCity Printers, 1977.

Clarke, Robin and Hindley, Geoffrey. *The Challenge of the Primitives.* New York: McGraw-Hill, 1975.

Duff, Wilson. *Images Stone B.C.: Thirty Centuries of Northwest Coast Indian Art.* Seattle: University of Washington Press, 1975.

Foest, Christian F. *Native Arts of North America.* New York: Oxford University Press, 1980.

Festivals and Celebrations, Engagement Calendar 1981, UNICEF.

Gardner, John. *On Moral Fiction.* New York: Basic Books, 1978.

Holm, Bill. *Crooked Beak of Heaven: Masks & Other Ceremonial Art of the Northwest Coast.* Seattle: University of Washington Press, 1972.

————. *Northwest Coast Indian Art: An Analysis of Form.* Seattle: University of Washington Press, 1965.

———— and Reid, Bill. *Indian Art of the Northwest Coast: A Dialogue on Craftsmanship & Aesthetics,* Houston: Institute for the Arts, Rice University, 1975.

Iglauer, Edith. *Inuit Journey.* North Vancouver, B.C.: Douglas & McIntyre, 1962.

Inuit Art in the 1970s. Kingston, Ontario: Agnes Etherington Art Centre, 1979.

The Inuit Artists of Inoucdjouac, P.Q. Historical & Biographical Information for the Viewers and Collectors of Eskimo Art. La Fédération des Cooperatives du Nouveau Quebec, etc., 1978.

The Inuit Artists of Sugluk, P.Q. La Fédération des Cooperatives du Nouveau Quebec, 1976.

The Inuit Print. Ottawa: National Museum of Man.

100 Years of Native American Painting. Oklahoma City: The Oklahoma Museum of Art, 1978.

The People Within: Art from Baker Lake. Art Gallery of Ontario, 1976.

Pike, Donald G. *Anasazi: Ancient People of the Rock.* New York: Crown Publishers, 1974.

Pitseolak. *Pictures Out of My Life,* from recorded interviews with Dorothy Eber. Seattle: University of Washington Press, 1971.

Ray, Dorothy Jean. *Eskimo Art: Tradition & Innovation in North Alaska.* Seattle: University of Washington Press, 1977.

Roy, Claude. *The Art of the Savages.* New York: Golden Griffin Books, 1958.

Sinclair, Lister and Pollock, Jack. *The Art of Norval Morrisseau.* London: Methuen, 1979.

Special Eskimo Art Issue, North-Nord. Ottawa, 1974.

Steltzer, Ulli. *Indian Artists at Work.* Seattle: University of Washington Press, 1976.

Turner, Lucien M. *Indians & Eskimos in the Quebec-Labrador Peninsula.* Quebec: Press Comeditex, 1979.

Wardwell, Allen. *Objects of Bright Pride.* New York: Center for Inter-American Relations, 1978.

We Lived by Animals. Montreal/Toronto: McClelland & Stewart, Ltd., 1971.

PART II

Arkus, Leon Anthony. *John Kane, Painter.* (Includes *Sky Hooks: The Autobiography of John Kane,* as told to Marie McSwigan.) Pittsburgh: University of Pittsburgh Press, 1971.

Bishop, Robert. *Folk Painters of America.* New York: E. P. Dutton, 1979.

———— and Coblentz, Patricia. *A Gallery of American Weathervanes and Whirligigs.* New York: E. P. Dutton, 1981.

Boyd, E. *Popular Arts of Spanish New Mexico.* Santa Fe: Museum of New Mexico Press, 1974.

Cahill, Holger; Barr, Alfred H.; et al. *Masters of Popular Painting.* New York: Museum of Modern Art, 1938.

Cahn, William. *Lawrence 1912: The Bread & Roses Strike.* New York: The Pilgrim Press, 1954.

Fried, Fred and Fried, Mary. *America's Forgotten Folk Arts.* New York: Pantheon Books, 1978.

Fuller, Edmund L. *Visions in Stone: The Sculpture of William Edmondson.* Pittsburgh: University of Pittsburgh Press, 1973.

Hemphill, Herbert W., Jr., and Weissman, Julia. *Twentieth Century American Folk Art and Artists.* New York: E. P. Dutton, 1974.

Horwitz, Elinor Lander. *Contemporary American Folk Artists.* Philadelphia and New York: J. B. Lippincott Co., 1975.

Janis, Sidney. *They Taught Themselves: American Primitive Painters of the Twentieth Century.* New York: Dial Press, 1942.

————, et al. *Morris Hirshfield.* Parma, Italy: Franco Maria Ricci, 1976.

Lichten, Frances. *Folk Art of Rural Pennsylvania.* New York: Charles Scribner's Sons, 1946.

Lipman, Jean and Armstrong, Tom. *American Folk Painting of Three Centuries.* New York: Hudson Hills Press and Whitney Museum of American Art, 1980.

Pileggi, Nicholas. *Portrait of the Artist* [Fasanella]. *New York Magazine,* October 30, 1972.

Rodman, Selden. *The Artist Nobody Knows* [Simon Radilla]. New York: New World Writing, 1952.

————. *Horace Pippin: A Negro Painter in America.* New York: Quadrangle Press, 1947.

———— and Cleaver, Carole. *Horace Pippin: The Artist as a Black American.* Garden City, N.Y.: Doubleday, 1972.

————. *Portrait of the Artist as an American* [Ben Shahn]. New York: Harper & Co., 1951.

Vogel, Donald and Vogel, Margaret. *Aunt Clara: The Paintings of Clara McDonald Williamson.* Austin: University of Texas Press and Amon Carter Museum of Western Art, 1966.

Watson, Patrick. *Fasanella's City: The Paintings of Ralph Fasanella with the Story of His Life and Art.* New York: Alfred A. Knopf, 1973.

Will Edmonson's Mirkels. Tennessee Fine Arts Center at Cheekwood, 1964.

PART III

Apraxine, Pierre. *Haitian Painting: The Naive Tradition.* New York: American Federation of Arts, 1973.

Art of Haiti and Jamaica. Stanton L. Catlin, Selden Rodman, DeWitt Peters. New York: Center for Inter-American Relations, 1968.

Bazin, Germain. *O Aleijadinho o a escultura barroca no Brazil.* Paris: Les Editions du Temps, 1963; Rio de Janeiro–Sao Paulo, 1971.

Malraux, André. *L'Intemporal.* Paris: Gallimard, 1978.

Rodman, Selden. *The Brazil Traveler: History, Culture, Literature and the Arts.* Old Greenwich, Conn.: Devin-Adair, 1975.

———. *Genius in the Backlands: Popular Artists of Brazil.* Old Greenwich, Conn.: Devin-Adair, 1977.

———. *Haiti: The Black Republic.* Old Greenwich, Conn.: Devin-Adair, 1978.

———. *Haitian Art: The Third Generation.* Norwalk, Conn.: MIND, 1979.

———. *Hyppolite's Heir: Lafortune Felix.* Washington, D.C.: *Américas,* September–October, 1982.

———. *The Miracle of Haitian Art.* Garden City, N.Y.: Doubleday, 1974.

———. *Renaissance in Haiti.* New York: Pellegrini & Cudahy, 1947.

———. *Sculptors of Haiti.* Washington, D.C.: *Américas.* October–November, 1981.

7 Brasileiros e seu universo. Catalogue to an exhibition of popular sculpture mounted by the Ministry of Education in Brasilia, 1974.

Stebich, Ute. *Haitian Art.* New York: Harry N. Abrams, Brooklyn Museum, 1978.

———. *Kunst aus Haiti.* Ulm, West Germany: International Primary Art GmbH.

Williams, Sheldon. *Voodoo and the Art of Haiti.* London: Morland Lee Ltd., 1971.

PART IV

Arts of the Cuna Indians. Washington, D.C.: Pan American Union, 1969.

Brownowski, Judith and Grant, Robert. *Artesanos Mexicanos.* Los Angeles: Craft & Folk Art Museum, 1978.

Charlot, Jean. *Art-Making from Mexico to China.* New York: Sheed & Ward, 1950.

Cordry, Donald. *Mexican Masks.* Austin: University of Texas Press, 1980.

——— and Cordry, Dorothy. *Mexican Indian Costumes.* Austin: University of Texas Press, 1968.

D'Harcourt, Raoul. *Primitive Art of the Americas.* Les Editions du Chene, New York: Tudor Publishing Company, 1950.

Dörner, Gerd. *Mexican Folk-Art.* Munich-Vienna: Wilhelm Andermann Verlag, 1962.

Ebersole, Robert P. *Folk Arts & Crafts of the Andes.* Gainesville: University Gallery, College of Fine Arts, University of Florida, 1978.

Ecuador: Hands, Light & Color: Ecuadorean Popular Art. Washington, D.C.: Interamerican Development Bank, 1980.

Giffords, Gloria Kay, *Mexican Folk Retablos, Masterpieces on Tin.* Tucson: University of Arizona Press, 1974.

Goldman, Shifra M. *Contemporary Mexican Painting in a Time of Change.* Austin: University of Texas Press, 1981.

Gostelow, Mary. *The Complete International Book of Embroidery.* New York: Simon & Schuster, 1977.

Lumholz, C. *Unknown Mexico.* 2 vols. New York, 1902.

———. *Symbolism of the Huichol Indians.* New York, 1907.

Menzie, Eleanor. *Hand Carved & Decorated Gourds of Peru.* Santa Monica, Calif.: Karneke Publishers, 1976.

Mexican Folk Arts. La Jolla, Calif.: The Art Center, 1963.

Mishima, Yukio. *The Sound of Waves.* New York: Alfred A. Knopf, 1954.

Molas from the San Blas Islands. New York: Center for Inter-American Relations, 1968.

Negrin, Juan. *The Huichol Creation of the World.* Sacramento, Calif.: Crocker Art Gallery, 1975.

Parker, Ann and Neal, Avon. *Molas, Folk Art of the Cuna Indians.* New York: Crown, 1977.

Pettersen, Carmen L. *Maya of Guatemala: Life and Dress.* Seattle: University of Washington Press and Ixchel Museum, Guatemala City, 1976.

Petterson, Richard. *Folk Art of Peru.* La Verne, Calif.: Preston Printing, 1968.

Rodman, Selden. *Marcial and His "Aztec" Family.* Norwalk, Connecticut: MIND, 1980.

———. *Mexican Journal: The Conquerors Conquered.* Old Greenwich, Conn.: Devin-Adair, 1957.

———. *The Mexico Traveler.* New York: Meredith Press, 1969.

———. *The Peru Traveler.* New York: Meredith Press, 1968.

———. *South America of the Poets.* New York: Hawthorn Books, 1970.

Sawyer, Alan R. *Ancient Peruvian Ceramics.* University Park, Penn.: Pennsylvania State University Museum, 1975.

Wafer, Lionel. *A New Voyage and Description of the Isthmus of America, 1699.* Cleveland, Ohio, 1903.

Whitaker, Irwin and Whitaker, Emily. *A Potter's Mexico.* Albuquerque: University of New Mexico Press, 1978.

Whitten, Norman. *Sacha Runa.* Urbana: University of Illinois Press, 1976.

Index
of
Persons

Italic page numbers refer to figures.

A

Achpacaja, Miguel, 179, *179*
Aeschlimann, Ralph, 52, *52*, colorplate 9
Alcanor, 138
Aleijadinho, 144–45, *145*, 149
Alvarado, Pedro de, 176
Ananaisee, 33, *33*
Anghik, Abraham Apakark, 51, *51*
Annanok, Thomassie, 42, *42*
Antonello da Messina, 114
Antunes, Nemesio, 188
Apollinaire, Guillaume, 90
Apraxine, Pierre, 146
Arkus, Leon Anthony, 62
Arp, Jean, 132
Astor, Mrs. Vincent, 123
Auden, W. H., 102
Augustin, Pierre, 135
Auxiliadora, Maria, 160, 161, *161*, *162*
Ayala, Juan Camilo, 201, 202, *202*, 204, colorplate 65
Ayala, Felix Camilo, 196, 201, 202, *202*
Ayala, Marcial, *see* Marcial

B

Baldwin, Frank, 60, 67–68, *67*, *68*, colorplate 21
Barbosa, José, 163–64, *163*
Barnes, Albert C., 76
Barr, Alfred, 70
Barragán, Luis, 165
Bazile, Castera, *2*, 115, 116, *116*, 121, 122, *122*, colorplate 35
Beardon, Romare, 77, 101
Beethoven, Ludwig van, 145, 196, 205, 206
Bemelmans, Ludwig, 184
Benoit, Rigaud, *2*, 13, 65, 111, 117, *117*, *118*, 119, *119*, 121, 122, *122*, colorplate 37, colorplate 38
Bigaud, Wilson, 119–21, *119*, *120*, *121*, 123, *123*, colorplate 36
Bihalji-Merin, Oto, 142
Blain, Roland, 136, colorplate 41
Blaise, St. Louis, 139, *139*, colorplate 44
Blake, William, 63
Blanchard, Smith, 135
Boas, Franz, 21, 25
Bombois, Camille, 67
Bosch, Hieronymus, 9

Bottex, J. B. and Seymour, 138
Brady, Robert, 201
Brancusi, Constantin, 19, 141, 189, 205
Breton, André, 104
Brewster, John, Jr., 58
Brierre, Murat, 126, *127*
Brinton, Christian, 72
Brown, John, 74
Brown, Lady Richmond, 170
Brueghel, Pieter, 72, 119, 195
Bruno, Giordano, 85
Buffalo Meat, 48, colorplate 14
Bunker, Ellsworth, 102
Butler, Jack and Sheila, 33, 35

C

Caboclo, Nhõ, 151–53, *152*, *153*, 154
Calder, Alexander, 42, 126, 152
Calfee, William, 122
Capote, Truman, 111
Caravaggio (Michelangelo Merisi), 27
Cardenal, Ernesto, 167, 168
Carlebach, Julius, 22–23
Carlen, Robert, 75–77
Carrilo, Tutukila, 194
Castaneda, Juan, 205
Cather, Willa, 13
Caudwell, Christopher, 94
Chael, 167, colorplate 61
Chapman, Isaac, 24
Chaverri, Joaquín, 179, *180*
Chex, Julian and Margarita, 179
Christophe, Henry, 106
Church, Henry, 60, 62–64, *62*, *63*, colorplate 18, colorplate 19
Coelho, Frota, Lelia, 160
Coleman, *60*
Cook, Captain James, 21
Cordry, Donald, 199
Cortez, Hernan, 176, 201
Covarrubias, Miguel, 199
Cranmer, Douglas, 26
Creek, Charlie, 86
Crowninshield, Frank, 62
Curuchic, Andrés, 178, *178*
Curuchic, Santiago, 179

D

Dahl-Wolfe, Louise, 70
Dalton, Brian, 43

Davidson, Robert, 26
Davies, Joseph, 58
Debs, Eugene V., 93
De Kooning, Willem, 116
Delfin, Victor, 187–89, *188, 189*
Deren, Maya, 125
Deschamps, Minnie, *77, 78, 79, 79,*
    colorplate 27
Desroches, Numa, *107*
Dimanche, André, 128
Djanira da Mota e Silva, 142, 144, 158,
    159, colorplate 47
Domond, Wilmino, 128, *129*
Dos Prazeres, Heitor, 142, *142,* 143,
    143, 144, *144,* 155
Duchamp, Marcel, 23
Dufaut, Préfèt, 123, colorplate 43
Duff, Wilson, 19, 25
Duperier, Odilon, 134
Duvalier, François, 124
Dvořák, Anton, 196

Fra Angelico, 114
Fried, Fred and Mary, 82
Fuller, Buckminster, 31

G

Gabriel, Ivan, 179
Gauguin, Paul, 63, 143
George, Charlie, 23
Gerson de Souza, 162–63, *162,* color-
    plate 49
Giotto, 62
Gonzales, Angel, 177, *177,* 179
Gourgue, Enguérrand, 128, *128,* 129,
    135, 136
Goya, Francisco, 9, 98, 195, 198
Gozzoli, Benozzo, 81
Graves, Morris, 54
GTO (Gerardo Telles de Oliveira), 13,
    149, *149,* 150, *150,* 151, *151,* 184, *184*
Guayasamín, Oswaldo, 184, *184*
Guillén, Asília, 167, 179–80
Guzman, Hector, 184–85, *185*
Gwathmey, Robert, 79

E

Eber, Dorothy, 39
Ebersole, Robert, 184
Edenshaw, Charles, 22, 24, 27
Edmondson, William, 9, 69–71, *69, 70,*
    71, 101
Emmons, George Thornton, 21, 24
Ernst, Max, 23
Euclid, 111
Evans, Minnie, *77,* 78, *78,* 79, color-
    plate 28
Evans, Walker, 79

H

Hamilton, Jane, 77
Hampton, James, 59, 85–87, *86, 87,*
    colorplate 26
Hawthorne, Nathaniel, 94
Haytor, S. W., 23
Healey, Giles Greville, 197
Hearst, William Randolph, 70
Heckel, Gustav, 155
Heye, George, 22
Hicks, Edward, 58, 67, 82
Hirsch, Sidney, 70
Hirshfield, Morris, 9, 89–90, *89, 91,*
    colorplate 24, colorplate 25
Hogarth, William, 82
Holm, Bill, 23, 24, 25, 31
Horwitz, Elinor Lander, 87
Houston, James, 32–33, 35, 39
Hugo, Victor, 102
Hugues, Victor, 102
Hyppolite, Hector, 12, 104–6, *105,*
    108–11, *109, 110,* 130, 148, *148,*
    colorplate 33

F

Fasanella, Ralph, 90–98, *94, 95, 96, 97,*
    colorplate 29, colorplate 30
Fasanella, Tess, 94
Faustin, Celestin, 135–36, *137*
Félix, Lafortune, 139, *139,* 140, *140,*
    colorplate 46
Field, Erastus Salisbury, 58–60, *58,*
    colorplate 16
Fils-Aimé, 139
Fisch, Olga, 182, 183
Fisher, Jonathan, 58, *59*
Flax, Walter, 86

I

Iaponi de Araujo Soares, 164, *164*
Iksiqtaaryuk/Kenak, 33, *36*
Inoséncio Jiménez Chino, *197, 202, 203*
Iracema Arditi, 155

J

Janis, Sidney, 89
Jannson, Erik, 60
Jean, Edner, 139
Jerôme, Jean-René, 140
Jiménez, Felix, *197,* 202–3, *203,* 204, colorplate 67
John, Alex, 129
Johnson, Lyndon B., 102
Jolimeau, Serge, 131, *131*
Joseph, Antonio, 140
Joseph, Jasmin, 128, 134
Joseph, Joseph, *80,* 81
Joseph, Nacius, 13, 132–35, *134, 135,* 148
Joyce, James, 9

K

Kandinsky, Wassily, 11
Kane, John, 60, *61,* 62, 76
Kapo (Mallica Reynolds), *102,* 103, *103*
Kenojuak Lukta, 40, *40*
Kingman, Eduardo, 184
Klee, Paul, 155
Krans, Olof, 60, *61*
Kuzshuktuk, 35

L

Lage, Eliane, 153
Lange, Dorothea, 79
Laratte, Georges, 132, *132,* 133, *133*
Larkin, Oliver, 55
Lawrence, Jacob, 77, 101
Lazoreck, Eve (Fasanella), 94
León, Noé, 168, *168,* 181
Levêque, Gabriel, 122
Levi-Strauss, Claude, 141, 158
Liautaud, Georges, 126, *126,* 127, *127,* 131, *131,* 147
Lipman, Jean, 57
Lopez, José Dolores, 50, *50,* colorplate 8
Lorenzetti, Ambrogio, 81
Louco (Boaventura da Silva), 145–49, *146, 147, 148*
Lowell, Robert, 102
Luck, Bernardo, 187
Lumholtz, Carl, 192, 193
Lynch, Laura, 88, *88,* colorplate 32

M

Malraux, André, 104, 129, 130
Marcantonio, Vito, 93
Marcial, Camilo Ayala, 12, 13, *13,* 167, 194–97, *195, 197,* 200–208, *201, 205, 206, 207, 208,* colorplate 64, colorplate 66, colorplate 68, colorplate 69
Martinez, Julian and Maria, 48
Martini, Simone, 114
Martins, Sylvia, 151, 152
Matta, Roberto, 23
Matthiessen, Peter, 194
Maurício, Roberto, *197, 203, 204*
McCarthy, Joseph, 90, 96
McCarthy, Pearl, 44
Metuso, Harvey, 96
Michelangelo Buonarotti, 9, 27
Miller, Arthur, 95
Mishima, Yukio, 207
Mompremier, Madsen, 135
Monnin, Michel, 132
Monosiet, Pierre, 133, 134
Mooney, Tom, 90
Morais, Crisaldo, 155
Morais, *see* Vinícius de Morais
Morales, António Viscara, *169*
Morales, Francisco Maydana, *169*
Morgan, Sister Gertrude, 86

Morrisseau, Norval, 13, 43–46, *43, 44, 45, 46,* 51, 188, colorplate 12, colorplate 13
Morse, Samuel F. B., 58
Moses, Anna M. R. (Grandma Moses), 64
Mozart, Leopold, 13
Mozart, Wolfgang Amadeus, 13, 23
Mozinha, 164, *164*

N

Naipaul, V. S., 102
Neal, Avon, 172, 174
Nearing, Scott, 93
Negrin, Juan, 193, 194
Negron, Bill, 171
Neruda, Pablo, 169, 188, 189
Neuton, Freitas de Andrade, 160, *161*
Nevelson, Louise, 85, 87
Newman, Barnett, 23
Newton, Isaac, 54
Niviaksiakik, 42, *42*
Nolde, Emil, 155

O

Obin, Antoine, 138
Obin, Henri-Claude, 138
Obin, Michel, 138, *138*
Obin, Philomé, *2,* 92, 111–16, *111, 112, 113, 115,* 120, 122, *122, 123,* 138, 147, 159
Obin, Senêque, 115, *115,* 138
Obin, Telemaque, 138
Olivier, Raymond, 140
Oonark, Jessie, 33, *33, 37*
Orozco, José Clemente, 184, 198, *198*

P

Parker, Ann, 172
Parra, Nicanor, 168
Parra, Violetta, 168–69, *169*
Parsons, Betty, 23
Paul, Damien, 126
Paul, Gerard, 135, *136*
Pedro II, 151, 159

Peters, DeWitt, 105, 108, 109, 121, 122, *122*
Pettersen, Carmen L., 175
Philippe-Auguste, Salnave, 128, *128,* 135, 136, colorplate 34
Phillips, Ammi, 58
Picasso, Pablo Ruiz, 9, 10, 17, 40, 41, 46, 90, 143, 199, 206
Pickett, Joseph, 60
Pierce, Elijah, 77
Pierre, André, 124–26, *124, 125, 126,* 136, colorplate 40
Pierre-Louis, Prosper, 130, *130,* colorplate 45
Pileggi, Nicholas, 95
Pippin, Horace, 9, 72–77, *72, 73, 74, 76, 77,* 92, 101, 143, 144, 159, colorplate 22, colorplate 23
Pitseolak Ashoona, 33, 38–40, *38,* 42, colorplate 10
Pizarro, Francisco, 181
Pluviose, Dieudonné, *114,* 138
Pollock, Jack, 43, 44, 51
Pontual, Roberto, 153
Posada, José Guadalupe, 198, *199*
Praxiteles, 17
Primitivo Evanon Poma, 186
Pudlo, 42, *42,* colorplate 59

R

Rabkin, Edmond and Carolyn, *197,* 200–205
Radilla, Simon, 81, 82–85, *83, 84,* 86
Rameau, Cameau, 136, 137, *138*
Reid, Bill, 13, 24, 25, 26–31, *27, 28, 29, 30,* 39, 44, 45, 51, colorplate 7
Rembrandt, 104
Rivera, Diego, 184, 198
Rocher, Camy, 135, 136, *136, 138*
Roosevelt, Eleanor, 71
Rosenberg, Sam, 62
Rosenberg, Ethel and Julius, 90, 96
Rousseau, Henri, 10, *10,* 11, 90, 128, 143, 144, 147, 155
Ryan, Terence, 39
Ryder, Albert Pinkham, 63

S

Sacco and Vanzetti, 90, 98
Sahagún, Padre, 190

St. Brice, Robert, 128, 129, *129*
Saint-Fleurant, Louisiane, 130, *130*
Sánchez, José Benítez, 193–94, *194,* colorplate 63
Sassetta, 151
Schoelcher, Victor, 102
Scholder, Fritz, 52, *52,* 53
Seaweed, Joe, 22
Seaweed, Willie, 23
Séjourné, Bernard, 140
Sengungetuk, Ronald, 51
Shahn, Ben, 79, 92, *92,* 94, 96, 98
Shapiro, Pauline, 88, *88,* colorplate 31
Shotridge, Louis, 22, *22*
Silva, Fernando V. da, 147, 160, *160,* colorplate 51
Silva, Maria Auxiliadora, *see* Auxiliadora
Silva, José Antonio da, 12, 142, 144, 153–58, *154, 155, 156, 157,* 160, colorplate 50
Silva, Julio Martins da, 159–60, *159, 160,* colorplate 48
Silverhorn, 48, *49*
Simil, Emilcar, 140
Simon, John, 141
Sinclair, Lester, 46
Sinvil, Michel, 132, 133, colorplate 39
Siqueiros, David Alfaro, 199
Sisana, Justo, 102, *102,* 103
Sparks, Esther, 60
Starr, Alfred and Elizabeth, 70
Steinberg, Saul, 42

T

Tahoma, Quincy, 48, colorplate 15
Tamayo, Rufino, 199
Tanguy, Yves, 23
Tavinick, 33
Titian, 104
Tobey, Mark, *37,* 54
Tookoome, 33, *37,* 40–42, *41,* colorplate 11
Tornawiecki, Juana, 187
Trujillo, Rafael Leonidas, 101
Tuctuc, Santiago, 179
Turnier, Luce, 140
Turulialik, 33

U

Ubico, Jorge, 175

V

Valcin, Gerard, 128
Van Gogh, Vincent, 63, 114
Vasari, Giorgio, 62
Velasquez, Diego, 198
Velasquez, José António, 167, *167,* 179, 180, *180*
Veronese, Paolo, 85
Versein, 132, 135, *135*
Vevers, 107, *108*
Villalba, Celestina, 187, *187*
Villalobos, Mário Tulio, 168, *168,* 181, colorplate 58
Vinícius de Morais, 143
Vital, Pauléus, 128, colorplate 42
Vitalino, 152, 153
Viteri, Oswaldo, 184, *184*
Voegeli, Bishop C. Alfred, 122, 123
Vogel, Donald and Margaret, 64, 65

W

Wafer, Lionel, 170
Wagner, Richard, 9, 13
Walcott, Derek, 102
Wardwell, Allen, 24, 26
Watson, Patrick, 94
Webb, Spider, 81
Wedges, F. A. Mitchell, 170
Weston, Edward, 70
Whitman, Walt, 58
Whitten, Norman, 182
Wiggins, David, 67, 68
Williamson, Clara (Aunt Clara), 60, 64–67, *64, 66*
Wilner, Jean, 138
Wilson, Mary Ann, 57, *66,* colorplate 20
Winchester, Alice, 57
Wyeth, N. C., 72

Y

Yucra, Victor, 186

Z

Zagar, Isaiah, 186
Zdaquira, Alberid, colorplate 60

Index of Works

Italic page numbers refer to figures.

A

Acrobats (Mexico), *191*
Adultery (Peru), *186–87*, *187*
advertisement for Wolcott's Instant Pain Annihilator, 1865 (U.S.), 63, *63*
Aida Wedo (Liautaud), *127*
America 1963 (Shapiro), 88, *88*, colorplate 31
Amish Letter Writer (Pippin), 73, *73*
Androgynous Fantasy (Jolimeau), *131*
Angel (Edmondson), 70, *71*
Angel in Tennis Shoes (Djanira), colorplate 47
Apostle Seamen (Louco), 148, *148*
Apparition (Haiti), *129*
Arbor Meeting (Williamson), 65, colorplate 20
Arrival of the Sun (Lutka), 40, *40*
Artist's Eye (Marcial), 205, *206*
Asleep (Pippin), *72*
Attack on Pioneers' Camp (U.S. West), 48, *49*

B

Bailán Combite (Achpacaja), *179*
Bal du Carnival (Benoit), 117, colorplate 37
Ball at the Court of King Henry Christophe (Blaise), *139*
Bandits Threatening Our Milpa (Chino), 202, *203*
bargaining for a zut (Guatemala), *175*
bark painting (Marcial), *201*
Baron Samedi (Félix), *140*
Barracks, The (Pippin), 73, 75, colorplate 23
Baseball: Night Game Practice (Fasanella), 96, *96*
Battle of Vertières (M. Obin), *138*
Bear Mother bowl (Reid), *29*
beaver memorial pole (Reid), *28*, colorplate 7
Benediction (Villalobos), *168*, colorplate 58
bentwood box (Tlingit), 24, *24*, colorplate 5
bird (Inuit), *36*
birdbath (Edmondson), *70*
Blind Leading the Blind, The (Brueghel), *195*

blind mask (Tsimshian region), 20, colorplate 1
Blue Crucifixion (Gerson), *162–63*, *162*
Boatmen (N. Joseph), *134*
Borboleta (J. M. da Silva), *159–60*, *160*
Bordello No. 1 (F. V. da Silva), colorplate 51
Bordello No. 2 (F. V. da Silva), *160*
Boss Politico as a Serpent (Posada), *199*
Both in Summer and Winter (Pitseolak), 38, *39*, colorplate 10
Building the Citadelle (Faustin), *137*
Bush-Negro home near Paramaribo (Surinam), *101*

C

Calice (Benoit), 119, *119*
Candomblé baptismal ceremony at a waterfall near Salvador (Brazil), *147*
Candomblé participants (Salvador da Bahia, Brazil), 146, *146*
candy skulls (Mexico), *190*
Centre d'Art jeep, DeWitt Peters at the wheel (Haiti), *122*
ceramic sculpture from Quinua (Peru), *185*
ceramic vessel from Sarayacu (Ecuador), *182*
ceremonial figures with bottles and necklaces (Rocher), *136*
Ceremony (Hyppolite), *110*
Ceremony for Ogoun (Vital), 128, colorplate 42
Ceremony for the Forest-God (Pierre), colorplate 40
Chicken for Dinner (Williamson), 65
Chilkat blankets (Tlingit), 21, *21*
Christophe Burning Cap Haïtien (Pluviose), *114*
Church Interior with Stained Glass (Fasanella), *95*
Church Service (Deschamps), colorplate 27
concrete bird (Delfin), *188*, *189*
Conflicts and Tensions (Bigaud), 120, *120*
Country and City (F. C. Ayala), *202*

cross (Liautaud), *127*

Crucified Christ (Louco), *147*

Crucifixion (Baldwin), 67–68, *67, 68*, colorplate 21

Crucifixion (Edmondson), *71*

Crucifixion (Hyppolite), *148*

Crucifixion (J. A. da Silva), 155, *156*

Crucifixion (P. Obin), 114, *122*

Crucifixion (Sinvil), colorplate 39

crucifixion mola (Cuna), colorplate 53

Crystal Palace, Rio de Janeiro (J. M. da Silva), colorplate 48

Cuna couple (Panama), *171*

Cuna Indian Woman (Panama), *170*

D

Dancer (Auxiliadora), *161, 162*

David Slaying the Lion (Domond), 128, *129*

Day the Bosque Froze Over, The (Williamson), *64*

Defense of the Duarte Bridge (Sisana), *102*

Delivery, The (Bazile), *116*

Demon-loa Riding a Cow (Brierre), *127*

Den, The (Pippin), 76, *77*

devil mask from Jaleaca, Guerrero (Mexico), colorplate 62

Devil Riding Dragon (Mexico), *199*

Dietitian of McGannon Hall, The (Edmondson), *71*

Discovery of My Girl (Mauricío), 204, *204*

Dismemberment of Tacutsi Nakawé (Sánchez), colorplate 63

Domino Players (Pippin), 73, colorplate 22

dragon transformation mask (Kwakiutl), 23–24, *24*

Dream, The (Marcial), 205, *206*

Dream of Motherhood (Pitseolak), 38, *42*

Dream of Times Past and Present, A (Marcial), 207

Dream Visions at the Edge of Darkness (Sánchez), *194*

E

early painting of Guédé retaining calabash shape (Pierre), 125, *125*

Earth Mother with Her Children (Morrisseau), *45*

Electricity Comes to Our Village (Marcial), 207, *208*

Elephant (Hirshfield), *91*

elephant-bath mola (Panama), 171, *172*

engraved gourds from Huancayo (Peru), *185*

Eve (Edmondson), *70*

Eve and the Crocodiles (Blain), colorplate 41

Execution of 3 May 1808 (Goya), 98, 195

F

facade of sign shop of Joseph Joseph (U.S.), *80, 81*

family group displaying fish (Inuit), *32*

Family in Rio Favela (Dos Prazeres), *144*

Family of Mermaids (Alkatukt), *33*

F. D. Roosevelt Interceding in the Beyond for the Peace of the Americas (P. Obin), *113*

felt and wool screen (Oonark), *33*

Fiesta (Ecuador), *183*

Fiesta (Villalba), 187, *187*

Fiesta (Zdaquira), colorplate 60

Fiesta en la Vida (Marcial), 205–6

Fiesta with Volcanoes and Angels (J. C. Ayala), 202, colorplate 65

Figure (Jolimeau), *131*

Figure (Oonark), *37*

Fish (Morrisseau), *44*

fisherman inflating sealskin (Inuit), *36*

Fisherman with Pail, Paddle and Traps (Annanok), 42, *42*

Fishing Village, Lake Nicaragua (Chael), 167, colorplate 61

Fish with Rider (Inuit), *35*

Flowers with Hat and Cane (Pippin), 73, *73*

formlines, painted screens and houseposts (U.S. Northwest Coast), 24, *26*

Funeral of Charlemagne Péralte (P. Obin), 112
Funeral Procession (Curuchic), 178

G

Garden of Eden (Lopez), 50
Getaway, The (Pippin), 75, 76
Giant Ring (GTO), 150, *150*
Girl in a Mirror (Hirshfield), 90, colorplate 24
Girl with a Dog (Hirshfield), colorplate 25
gold bracelet with dogfish motif (Reid), 27
gold casket (Reid), 29, *29*
Gray Day (Fasanella), 96–98, *97*, colorplate 30
grizzly bear (Reid), *28*
Guardian of the Egg (Aeschlimann), 52, *52*, colorplate 9
Guernica (Picasso), 46

H

hafted hammer (U.S. Northwest Coast), 19, *19*, 25
Haida Village Project (Reid), *28*
hand hammer (Alaska), 19, *19*
Hanging My Critics (J. A. da Silva), 154–55, *154*
Harbor and Streets of Jacmel (Du-Faut), 123, colorplate 43
hardware-shop sign in Chichicastenango (Guatemala), *175*
Hawk that Eats Whales, The (U.S. Northwest Coast), 19, *19*, 25
Hermaphroditic Demon (Liautaud), 127
Hinchaway (Poma), 186, colorplate 59
Historical Monument of the American Republic (Salisbury), 58, *58*, colorplate 16
Holy Mountain (Pippin), 73, 77
Holy Mountain No. 2 (Pippin), 77, *77*
horse (Sioux), *18*
Houngan, The (Rameau), 138
Huichol Indian with face-paint, parrot-feather cape, and woven belts (Mexico), *193*
huipil (Guatemala), 175, colorplate 56

I

"Ici la Renaissance" bar in Montrouis (Haiti), 105, *106*
Images of Vaudou (Pierre), 124
In a Time of Plenty (Tookoome), 40, 41, 42, colorplate 11
Incident in the War of the Pacific (Parra), 169, *169*
incised pipestem (Alaskan Eskimo), *32*
Indian (Caboclo), 152, *153*
Indian blanket of llama wool depicting astronauts (Peru), 186, *186*
Indians burning pagan copal at Catholic church (Guatemala), *176*
Indians in traditional costumes in the village of Nahualá (Guatemala), *167*
insects with "god's eyes" (Mexico), *193*
Interrupted Marriage, The (Benoit), 117, *117*
In the Days of Plenty (Tahoma), 48, colorplate 15
iron mask (Delfin), 189, *189*

J

Jesus Is My Airplane (Morgan), 86
Jezebel (Edmondson), *69*
Joe, the Iceman, No. 4 (Fasanella), 93, *94*
John Brown Going to His Hanging (Pippin), 73, 74, *74*
John Brown Reading His Bible (Pippin), 73, 74–75, *74*
Jonah and the Whale (Paul), 136

K

Kachina doll (Hopi), *48*
King and Eye, The (Gerson), 163, colorplate 49
Kite Flyers (Neuton), *161*

L

lady has lost her shawl and the shawl is weeping for the lady, The (Marcial), 203
Landscape with Peasant Farmers (J. A. da Silva), 154
Laughing Indian (Scholder), 52
Legendary Scroll Motifs (Morrisseau), 43
Lily of the Mohawk, The (Morrisseau), 44
Loas (Pierre-Louis), 130, colorplate 45
Lovers (Chino), 203, 203, colorplate 67
Lovers (Laratte), 133
Lucifer mask and devil-dance costume (A. V. Morales and F. M. Morales), 168, 169

M

Magic Table, The (Gourgue), 128, 128
Maîtresse la Sirène (Pierre), 126
Mambo (Rocher), 138
Mambo with Flowers (Saint-Fleurant), 130
Mambo with Telephone Poles (Félix), 140, colorplate 46
Man Carrying Reluctant Wife (Pudlo), 42, 42
Man on Bicycle Delivering Laundry (Dos Prazeres), 144
Mardi-Gras celebrant (Panama), 100
Marimaid (Wilson), 57
Market (Marcial), 201
Marriage at Cana, The (Bigaud), 123, 123
mask (Mexico), 199
mask (Tlingit), colorplate 6
masked figure in devil dance (Bolivia), 186, colorplate 52
mask with abalone-shell inlay (Bella Bella-Haida), 23, 23
Maya Indian wearing a huipil (Guatemala), 176
Maya mural at Tikal (Guatemala), 177
Mermaid from Guerrero (Mexico), 192
Mermaid from Metepec (Mexico), 192
metal staff with *candomblé* symbols from Salvador da Bahia (Brazil), 147
Metamorphis of the Sea Loa (N. Joseph), 134, 134
Migration (Orozco), 198

Miners (Djanira), 159
Mobile (Caboclo), 152, 153
molas (Cuna), 170, 170, 174
Monkey Picture, The (Church), 62, 63–64, 63, colorplate 19
Moros (Gonzalez), 176, 177, 177
Moses and Aaron (Hirshfield), 91
Mother and Child (Marcial), 13, 206
Mounted Ogoun (Hyppolite), 110
Mourning Figures (Versein), 135
muñecas (Mexico), 201
mural at Croix-des-Missions (Pierre), 125
mural on parking lot wall (U.S.), 82, 82
Murder in the Jungle (N. Joseph), 134, 134
Musicians (Chex), 178
Musk Ox (Tookoome), 37

N

Nativity (Benoit), 122
Nativity (P. Obin), 115
Navajo Indian sand-painters at work (U.S.), 47
Nocturnal Fiesta (Marcial), 195, 195, 196, colorplate 64
Nuestra Señora de la Luz (Lopez), 50, colorplate 8

O

oil study for Washington Social Security Building mural (Shahn), 92
O Jabú (Caboclo), 152
Old Man in Thought (Marcial), 205, 205
One, Walk through the Seasons (Marcial), 207
On the Fence (Deschamp), 79
Our Village (Marcial), 195, 195

P

painted cart (Chaverri), 180
painted wooden birds (Haiti), 183
painting (Evans), colorplate 28
painting (Guyasamín), 184
painting (Viteri), 184

painting on tailgate mud-flap of truck in Tio favela (Brazil), 163, *163*
Papa Zaca (Bigaud), colorplate 36
Park Bench, The (Pippin), 73
Peaceable Kingdoms (Hicks), 58
Peasant Family (Bazile), 116, colorplate 35
pendant (Canada), colorplate 3
penguin TV ad and mola derived from it (Panama), 172, *173*
People of the Potlatch (Reid), 27
pictographs on peasant *caille* near Jeremie (Haiti), 106, *106*
Pleasures of Eating Fish (Tookoome), *41*
Polar Bear and Cub on Ice (Niviaksiakik), 42, *42*
polychrome wood and metal (Santo), colorplate 57
Portrait of Mme. Antenor Firmin (P. Obin), 115
postage stamps, four Northwest Coast Indian masks (U.S.), 23, *23*
pottery with reliefs (Raquirá), 181
pre-Columbian skull frieze at Chichén-Itzá (Mexico), *190*
Preparation of Corn (Marcial), 205
Priest and Jaguar (León), 168
Procession (Mexico), 198
Procession to the Mountain (J. C. Ayala), *202*
Prophets at Church of Bom Jesus (Aleijadinho), 145, *145*

Q

Quadruhuaq, The Mysterious Helper (Tookoome), 43–44, *43*

R

Racho (Caboclo), 152, *153*
Raven Discovering Mankind in the Clamshell (Reid), 30, *31*
Reconciliation (Kapo), *103*
Relief with Symbols (N. Joseph), 135, *135*
Retablo (Mexico), *191*
Revolutionary Cabinet of 1915 Awaiting Arrival of Wounded (P. Obin), 113
robe, shark with monsters (Tlingit), colorplate 4

S

Sacrifice of the Cock (Bigaud), *120*
Ste. Trinité, apse of the Cathedral (Haiti), *2*, 114, 122, *122*, *123*
St. George Exorcising a Demon (Iaponi), 164, *164*
Sans Souci Palace (Desroches), 105–6, *107*
screen (Reid), 29, *29*
Sea Goddess (Iemanja) Lifted from Waves (Louco), 148–49, *148*
Seated Woman (Benoit), colorplate 38
Seduction for Treasure (Faustin), 136, *137*
Self-Portrait (Buffalo Meat), 48, colorplate 14
Self-Portrait (Church), 62, *62*, *63*, colorplate 18
Self-Portrait (Dos Prazeres), *143*
Self-Portrait (Fisher), *59*
Self-Portrait (Hirshfield), *89*
Self-Portrait (J. A. da Silva), 157, *157*
Self-Portrait (Kane), 60, *61*
Self-Portrait (Krans), 60, *61*
Self-Portrait (Marcial), *201*, 205, colorplate 66
Self-Portrait (Morrisseau), *43*, colorplate 12
Self-Portrait in Mardi Gras Costume (Bigaud), 121, *121*
Shaman (Iksiktaaryuk), 36
Shaman in Transformation (Anghik), 51, *51*
Shaman with Spirit Helpers (Morrisseau), *46*
Shipibo potters with ceramic vessel (Peru), *183*
ship-prow carving (Brazil), 163, *163*
Shipwreck, The (Benoit), 118, *118*
Sinking of the Titanic (U.S.), colorplate 17
Sleigh-Ride (Hirshfield), *91*
Small Figure with Rings (GTO), 148–49, *149*
Snake Goddess (Hyppolite), *109*
Solomon's Temple (Evans), *78*
space vehicle mola (Panama), 172–74, colorplate 54
Spirit of Winter (U.S. Northwest Coast), *34*
Stations of the Cross (J. A. da Silva), 155, colorplate 50
Stations of the Cross at Congonhas (Aleijadinho), 145, *145*
stone heads (Laratte), 132
stone masks (Tsimshian region), 20, *20*

Street-Car at Waxachie (William-son), *66*

string-animated calaveras (Mexico), *190*

subway sketch on copy of *New York Times* (Fasanella), *94*

Sunday Morning (J. A. da Silva), 155, *155*

Swimmers (J. A. da Silva), 155, *156*

T

Tailor-Made Girl (Hirshfield), *91*

tattooed lady (Webb), *81*

Tennis Match (Pitseolak), 42

Tenue à l'Extraordinaire (S. Obin), *115*

Three Brothers, Old Head-men of the Chilkat Tribe (Case and Draper), *21*

Three-Eyed King, The (Hyppolite), colorplate 33

three mola-wearing Cunas (Panama), *173*

Three Mysterious Women, The (Benoit), *117*

Three Queens (St. Brice), *129*

Throne of the Third Heaven of the Nations Millennium General Assembly (Hampton), 59, 85–87, *86*, *87*, colorplate 26

Tile Setter (Djanira), *159*

Tilted Landscape (Marcial), 207, *207*

Time of the Gourds, The (Blaise), *139*, colorplate 44

tobacco mortar (beaver) (prehistoric Haida), *25*

transformation mask (Kwakiutl), 24, *24*

Tree of Life, The (Liautaud), *127*

Trésors de Reine Titane (DuFaut), *124*

trial mural in library of old Centre d'Art (P. Obin), 122, *123*

tribal Indian conglomerate (GTO), 150–51, *150*

Triptych, Church of São Bom Jesús (GTO), 149, *149*

Triumph (Bazile), *116*

two figures in white stone (Laratte), *133*

two figures on a bowl (Mimbres), *47*, colorplate 2

Two Mermaids (Philippe-Auguste), *128*, colorplate 34

typical dwelling in the Ayalas' village (Mexico), *197*

V

vevers (Haiti), 107, *108*

View from Maggie's Window, The (Lynch), 88, *88*, colorplate 32

View of San António de Oriente (Velásquez), 179, *180*

Virgin Standing on a Lamb (N. Joseph), 135, *135*

Virgin with Penitent Angels (Louco), 147–48, *147*

W

Wall Street (Fasanella), 95, colorplate 29

War (Rousseau), *10*

Warrior with Thunderbirds (Morrisseau), colorplate 13

Watts Towers (Radilla), 83, *83*, *85*

Wave, The (Marcial), 206, *207*, colorplate 68

Wedding at Home (Mozinho), 164, *164*

Whale House screen (Tlingit), 22, *22*

Whaling Off the Coast of California (Coleman), *60*

What the Sun Sees (Marcial), 208, *208*, colorplate 69

White Sands (Williamson), *66*

Witch, The (Maurício), 203–4, *204*

Woman Carrying Her Crippled Husband (Liautaud), *131*

Women Planting Corn (Krans), 60, *61*

wool devil mask of Imbabura (Ecuador), 181–82, *182*

Y

Young Kiowa Brave (Silverhorn), 48, *49*

Z

Zingarella (Fasanella), *97*, 98

zut (Guatemala), 175, colorplate 55

Photo Credits

by illustration number

About the Author

Selden Rodman's career as a nonconformist in the arts began at Yale and has continued to the present with his championship of the Haitian, Brazilian and Mexican popular artists. His first art book, *Horace Pippin: A Negro Artist in America* (1947), was also the first book ever written about a black artist. The following year *Renaissance in Haiti*, the first of five books on Haiti, helped launch the world's most famous popular art movement. And the year after that Rodman initiated and directed the mural painting of the Cathedral Ste. Trinité in Port-au-Prince by eight self-taught Haitian artists. *Genius in the Backlands* (1977) and *Marcial and His "Aztec" Family* (1980) were the first studies of popular art in Brazil and Mexico. Rodman's interviews with artists and writers, *Conversations with Artists* (1957) and *Tongues of Fallen Angels* (1974), established a new genre in reporting, and his wide-ranging *The Caribbean* (1968) and *South America of the Poets* (1970) were a new kind of travel book. The poet and art critic lives with his wife and three children in Oakland, New Jersey, and Jacmel, Haiti.